# Popular Communication, Piracy and Social Change

Digital piracy cultures and peer-to-peer technologies combined to spark transformations in audio-visual distribution between the late 1990s and the mid-2000s. Digital piracy also inspired the creation of a global anti-piracy law and policy regime, and counter-movements such as the Swedish and German Pirate Parties. These trends provide starting points for a wide-ranging debate about the prospects for deep and lasting changes in social life enabled by piratical technology practices. This edited volume brings together contemporary scholarship in communication and media studies, addressing piracy as a recombinant feature of popular communication, technological innovation, and communication law and policy. An international collection of contributors highlights key debates about piracy, popular communication, and social change, and provides a lasting resource for global media studies.

This book was originally published as a special issue of *Popular Communication: The International Journal of Media and Culture*.

**Jonas Andersson Schwarz** is Senior Lecturer in Media and Communication at Södertörn University, Sweden. He specializes in digital media cultures and technologies, and how these are structurally conditioned.

**Patrick Burkart** is Professor of Communication at Texas A&M University, College Station, TX, USA. He researches information law and policy, political economy, and popular communication, and is co-editor-in-chief of *Popular Communication: The International Journal of Media and Culture*.

# Popular Communication, Piracy and Social Change

**Edited by**
**Jonas Andersson Schwarz and**
**Patrick Burkart**

Routledge
Taylor & Francis Group

LONDON AND NEW YORK

First published 2017 by Routledge

2 Park Square, Milton Park, Abingdon, Oxfordshire OX14 4RN
711 Third Avenue, New York, NY 10017

*Routledge is an imprint of the Taylor & Francis Group, an informa business*

First issued in paperback 2018

*British Library Cataloguing in Publication Data*
A catalogue record for this book is available from the British Library

ISBN 13: 978-1-138-20419-5 (hbk)
ISBN 13: 978-0-367-03005-6 (pbk)

Typeset in Times New Roman
by RefineCatch Limited, Bungay, Suffolk

**Publisher's Note**
The publisher accepts responsibility for any inconsistencies that may have
arisen during the conversion of this book from journal articles to book chapters,
namely the possible inclusion of journal terminology.

**Disclaimer**
Every effort has been made to contact copyright holders for their permission to
reprint material in this book. The publishers would be grateful to hear from any
copyright holder who is not here acknowledged and will undertake to rectify
any errors or omissions in future editions of this book.

# Contents

# Citation Information

The following chapter was originally published in *Popular Communication: The International Journal of Media and Culture*, volume 9, issue 2 (May 2011). When citing this material, please use the original page numbering for each article, as follows:

**Chapter 1**
*Mobility Through Piracy, or How Steven Seagal Got to Malawi*
Jonathan Gray
*Popular Communication: The International Journal of Media and Culture*, volume 9, issue 2 (May 2011), pp. 99–113

The following chapters were originally published in *Popular Communication: The International Journal of Media and Culture*, volume 13, issue 1 (March 2015). When citing this material, please use the original page numbering for each article, as follows:

**Introduction**
*Piracy and Social Change*
Jonas Andersson Schwarz and Patrick Burkart
*Popular Communication: The International Journal of Media and Culture*, volume 13, issue 1 (March 2015), pp. 1–5

**Chapter 2**
*"Honorable Piracy" and Chile's Digital Transition*
Jennifer Ashley
*Popular Communication: The International Journal of Media and Culture*, volume 13, issue 1 (March 2015), pp. 6–17

**Chapter 3**
*Piracy, Geoblocking, and Australian Access to Niche Independent Cinema*
Rebecca Beirne
*Popular Communication: The International Journal of Media and Culture*, volume 13, issue 1 (March 2015), pp. 18–31

For any permission-related enquiries please visit:
http://www.tandfonline.com/page/help/permissions

# Notes on Contributors

**Jonas Andersson Schwarz** is Senior Lecturer in Media and Communication at Södertörn University, Sweden. He specializes in digital media cultures and technologies, and how these are structurally conditioned.

**Jennifer Ashley** is Assistant Professor in the Faculty of Global Affairs, George Mason University, Washington D.C., USA. Her work examines media and social movements in Latin America.

**Rebecca Beirne** is Senior Lecturer in the School of Humanities and Social Science, University of Newcastle, Australia. Her work examines lesbian representation in popular culture. She is co-editor of *Making Film and Television Histories* (2011) and *Televising Queer Women* (2007).

**Patrick Burkart** is Professor of Communication at Texas A&M University, College Station, TX, USA. He researches information law and policy, political economy, and popular communication, and is co-editor-in-chief of *Popular Communication: The International Journal of Media and Culture*.

**Luke Goode** is Associate Professor in Film, Television and Media Studies at the University of Auckland, New Zealand. His work examines the social and cultural impacts of changes in media culture and technology. His articles have appeared in journals such as *Media, Culture and Society* and *Popular Communication: The International Journal of Media and Culture*.

**Jonathan Gray** is Professor of Media and Cultural Studies at the University of Wisconsin-Madison, USA. His research interests include textual theory, contemporary television studies, new media extensions of television and film, and international media consumption. He has published widely in his field, including *A Companion to Media Authorship* (2013) and *Breaking Boundaries in Political Entertainment Studies* (2013).

**Justin Lewis** is Assistant Professor of English at the University of Nevada, Reno, USA. His research interests include technical communication, digital writing, database architecture, and intellectual property. His work has appeared in journals such as *Enculturation* and *Popular Communication: The International Journal of Media and Culture*.

**Jeremy Wade Morris** is Assistant Professor of Media and Cultural Studies at the University of Wisconsin-Madison, USA. His areas of expertise include digital music, music streaming services, cloud computing, and business method patents.

NOTES ON CONTRIBUTORS

**Jörgen Skågeby** is Associate Professor of Media and Cultural Studies at Stockholm University, Sweden. His research interests include media archaeology, cultural attunement, media temporalities, and media sharing. His most recent publications can be found in the *International Journal of Media and Culture* and *First Monday*.

# INTRODUCTION

## Piracy and Social Change

Jonas Andersson Schwarz
*Södertörn University*

Patrick Burkart
*Texas A&M University*

As guest editors for this special issue on piracy and social change, we re-engage a line of inquiry in critical media studies on popular communication begun in prior issues of *Popular Communication*. This journal's previous editors and contributors have already recognized the role of piracy in altering media economics and in promoting cultural reproduction in ways that promote or suppress the popularization of certain kinds of communication. Bielby and Harrington (2010), for example, noted how piracy alters TV marketing strategies, while Baym (2010, 2011) linked piracy to a general retooling of music for export markets and Adejunmobi (2011) linked piracy to deflationary economics in national film industries. Text-centered approaches have assessed how piracy assists popular communication by increasing the diffusion and impacts of cultural texts and paratexts (Gray, 2011; Pearson, 2010). Since then, Castells and Cardoso (2012) solicited cultural studies research on the topic of piracy in another journal, the *International Journal of Communication*, and even more recent books on the subject (Andersson Schwarz, 2013; Burkart, 2014) add new facets to social studies of piracy. This special issue on piracy and social change presents new popular communication scholarship as seen "through the prism of world events and their underlying dynamics" (Burkart & Christensen, 2013, p. 3) and using a variety of scholarly perspectives.

In much communication research, online file sharing is still approached as a novel form of media distribution and consumption, yet it underlies the rationale for the Internet protocol suite; it is now more than 15 years since Napster's emergence as a commercial platform for file sharing (Nowack & Whelan, 2014), and infamous sites such as The Pirate Bay have entered a decade or more of existence. The turn from legal studies to critical communication literature on piracy occurred around the turn of the millennium. A basic challenge persists for the field—to track a phenomenon that is vast, heterogeneous, and maybe even inherently nebulous. To take stock, we need to consider a wide range of research on sharing and piracy and relate it systematically to forms and expressions of social agency, including political conflict, class conflict, and cultural conflict. The analytical challenge grows as digital media infrastructures develop to permit "the unrestricted duplication of digitized media content between autonomous end-nodes on the Internet" (Andersson Schwarz, 2013, p. 2). For the networks described by our contributors in this issue, the everyday use and practices of piracy are irrevocably intertwined with material infrastructures and socio-technical structures.

Scholarship on piracy and pirates has changed in tone since the Napster watershed, partly in recognition of the fact that "pirate" culture and everyday culture increasingly mix in popular communication. Piracy scholarship reflects consumption norms that transgress legally proscribed orders, while the "piracy" label in politics and public relations is still used to shore up support for entrenched political and economic interests. For this special issue, we solicited contributions taking a novel and inquisitive approach to piracy and popular communication, while also mapping the current state of the field. Contributors were asked to focus on one or more communicative aspects of piracy, such as pirate cultures, practices, politics, aesthetics, ethics, law and policy, and modernities. We have endeavored to bring together pieces which explore the linkages between practices that could be deemed "piratical" or transgressive, their relationship to popular communication, and their contribution to social change or stasis.

The six contributions we have chosen for this special issue, in addition to the roundtable discussion accompanying them, bring together topics related to identity, access, and social structures. Several remind us that digital piracy is a contemporary phenomenon, premised on fast-moving technological change, but also carrying inherited links to historical counterparts. An interpretive historicity is still required, in spite of the imminent aspects of networking trends and techniques. The principal tendencies have historical precedents which are important to keep in mind. Media history becomes essential for developing a "media archeology" (Skågeby, this issue), for reflection on new business models built on file-sharing (Morris, this issue), and for law and policy studies (Ashley, this issue).

The concern to relate a contemporary history of piracy with inherited forms of civic expression is identified with a political sensibility toward "online ecology," which is in turn partially a response to the transnationalization of the US "copyfight." Pirate identity politics (reflected in kopimism, hacktivism, and demoscenes) unfold dialectically alongside the harmonization of national IP laws with European directives and transnational treaties. At even a material level, the technological potentials which charge online piracy can contribute discursively and pragmatically to the promises, fears, and expectations which envelop the phenomenon and so shape the coordination of social action. User reflexivity in online file sharing can thereby contribute directly to new social dynamics (Andersson Schwarz, 2013).

Ashley's (this issue) media history explores pirate modes of operation of Chile's broadcasting history during Pinochet's regime (1973–1990). Media activists used what they called "honorable piracy" for radical media aimed at restoring democracy. After the fall of the regime, a similar argument for honorable piracy has been utilized by community television participants in order to rationalize their unauthorized transmissions of alternative programming to low-income households. More recently, the transition to digital broadcasting has allowed these civic media activists the possibility of redefining democratic access to the public sphere and attaining legal recognition.

Access to media likewise characterizes the focus of Beirne's (this issue) exposition of geoblocking Australians' access to niche independent cinema, and "pirate" modes of exchange of lesbian films. These contributions enrich our understanding of not only alternative media systems and national access policies, but also of the normative dimensions of infrastructure policy and the socio-technical construction of media distribution. They also explore piracy as a component in a wider field of structural change in media consumption, distribution, and production.

The contributions by Morris (this issue) and by Lewis (this issue) take a platform-based approach to the history of dedicated infrastructural systems for file sharing such as Napster. Morris attunes us to the latent contradictions inherent to p2p-based file sharing, by reading the history of Napster as a means of capitalist production of value. He considers the case of audience measurement company BigChampagne as an early example of a back-end, server-based institutional actor who acts as an "infomediary," generating a cybernetic commodity of ratings from inferences about audience preferences, even in seemingly non-commercial systems for "free" exchange such as Napster. Lewis's article is part of the growth of media audience scholarship that explores the attitudes, norms, and beliefs of active file sharers. By interpreting systemically the tropes expressed by file sharers in various online forums, differences in community standards among file sharers are revealed, and—more importantly—mainstream presuppositions of piratical motivations are challenged. Lewis provides new clues about the transition in progress from illegitimate modes of consumption (p2p file sharing) to legitimate ones (streaming).

While Lewis explores the file-sharer ethos, Goode (this issue) analyzes dialectically the ethos inherent in the infamous Anonymous movement. An ethos, in this sense, could be understood as a shared set of not only political and ethical values, but the behavior, character, and disposition of political actors, and the ways in which these are projected. Undoubtedly, the pirate ethos shares with Anonymous a foundationalist belief in digitization as a progressive force. The roots of both movements are, in a sense, prepolitical, stemming from a pranksterist, playful adoption of technology in the service of political activism and culture jamming. Goode provides an ideological analysis of the hacktivism and adversarial stance of Anonymous towards authorities both offline and online, emphasizing rhizomatic, shape-shifting features which obscure identities. Anonymous should not be thought of as an appreciably coherent force; it ostensibly contains both (proto)socialist and libertarian energies, but its real shared heritage lies more in its carnivalesque, pluralist heritage, Goode argues.

Both Anonymous and digital piracy activism could be thought of as novel forms of pluralist cosmopolitanism. Just as file sharers routinely express a certain espousal of the "Pandora's box" of digitization (i.e., the simple observation that on the internet, a leaked piece of content, no matter how minimal, will potentially be duplicated, multiplied, and dispersed; see Andersson Schwarz, 2013, p. 23) there is an assertion of openness and dispersion also in Anonymous' affirmation of the "Streisand effect" (i.e., the observation that once leaked onto the internet, popular stories cannot be suppressed). Both groups advocate strong individualist discretion in terms of what rights citizens should have in terms of accessing and re-distributing media content. This radical individualism is, however, in a tension with the hive-mind collectivism also found in these movements. Still, just as Anonymous does not really employ deliberative consensus-building, but rather employ ad hoc, swift "swarming" (Goode, this issue), pirate collectivism neglects actively inclusionary "push" logics in favor of a "pull" logic (Andersson Schwarz, 2013, p. 17). If you are not independent enough and quick enough on your feet to join the swarm, Anonymous seems to tell us, you will not be guaranteed inclusion or access to the community.

The contributors to this special issue remind us that there is both a two-track and a hybrid distribution system evolving for digital distribution. Despite ascendant legal streaming sites, significant numbers of internet users have kept consuming copyrighted content in illicit ways, accessing ample and user-friendly file hosting sites ("cyberlockers") as well as unlicensed "pirate" streaming sites. Alongside a privatization of online sociality, where actors such as Facebook, Google, and Twitter control what is permissible on their platforms for user interaction, unregulated file sharing still informs basic expectations about media consumption and is a structural referent among many fans of popular culture ("I could just as well download this" the reasoning goes; hence the impracticality of measures such as geoblocking). Further, many of the popular forms of media consumption today, such as video viewing on YouTube, rely on a grey zone of copyright where content has been posted without remuneration to the formal rights holders. There appears to be considerable momentum for the monetization of clips as yet uncleared for copyright (Garrahan, 2014). The traditional militancy of the ongoing copyfight continues to find expression in populist movements online, but is being tempered by broad participation in both hybrid and parallel pirate practices.

The historical continuum of mainstream and hacker-based practices of piracy is also demonstrated by Skågeby's (this issue) article, which documents how Swedish public service radio experimented with broadcasting user-generated computer code in the mid-1980s. Both Skågeby and Ashley discuss "piracy" as a structural feature of media systems that public-service broadcasters are forced to deal with—either, as in Ashley's case, in actively promoting change or, as in Skågeby's case, as an anachronistic "intermediality" in the digital transition of mass media. Skågeby describes an early stage of the Swedish digital transition to have been an imagined "computer world" emerging with the help of computer software propagated by the government-owned broadcasting network over analog frequencies and copied by audience members onto old-fashioned cassette tapes.

It is worth noting early that Sweden is the home of infamous file sharing sites such as The Pirate Bay and also to legal streaming services such as Spotify, which have been embraced as The Pirate Bay's legitimate successors (a development that serves as a reference point in several of the articles). The recent, large migration of internet users from unregulated p2p-based file sharing to sanitized, corporate-owned streaming platforms such as Spotify, Pandora, and Netflix follows technology developments informed, at least to some degree, by the many Swedish experiences with file sharing through the last decade.

Finally, in recognition that celebratory discourses on piracy can compete with counter-discourses intended to reform practices of copyright maximalism, we address fair use at length in the roundtable discussion with legal scholars (Patricia Aufderheide and Peter Jaszi) and ethnographers of internet culture (Christopher Kelty and Gabriella Coleman; see Andersson Schwarz et al., this issue). Although we note that the legal traditions of fair use are far more robust in the United States than in Europe or the rest of the world, we hope that the roundtable further broadens the discussion of media piracy beyond purely juridical or political interpretations of access, to also address the aesthetics and ethics of cultures oriented to sharing media without the permission of copyright owners.

## REFERENCES

Adejunmobi, M. (2011). Nollywood, globalization, and regional media corporations in Africa. *Popular Communication*, *9*(2), 67–78.

Andersson Schwarz, J. (2013). *Online file sharing: Innovations in media consumption.* New York, NY: Routledge.

Baym, N. K. (2010). Rethinking the music industry. *Popular Communication*, *8*(3), 177–180.

Baym, N. K. (2011). The Swedish model: Balancing markets and gifts in the music industry. *Popular Communication*, *9*(1), 22–38.

Bielby, D., & Harrington, C. L. (2010). Global TV 2010. Update of the world markets for television. *Popular Communication*, *8*(3), 217–221.

Burkart, P. (2014). *Pirate politics: The new information policy contests.* Cambridge, MA: The MIT Press.

Burkart, P., & Christensen, M. (2013). Geopolitics and the popular. *Popular Communication*, *11*(1), 3–6.

Castells, M., & Cardoso, G. (2012). Piracy cultures: Editorial introduction. *International Journal of Communication*, *6*, 812–833.

Garrahan, M. (2014, October 13). YouTube pays out $1bn to producers by selling ads on copyrighted videos. *Financial Times* [London], p. 15.

Gray, J. (2011). Mobility through piracy, or how Steven Seagal got to Malawi. *Popular Communication*, *9*(2), 99–113.

Nowack, R., & Whelan, A. (Eds.). (2014, October). Napster, 15 years on: Rethinking digital music distribution. *First Monday*, *19*(10).

Pearson, R. (2010). Fandom in the digital era. *Popular Communication*, *8*, 84–95.

# Mobility Through Piracy, or How Steven Seagal Got to Malawi

Jonathan Gray

*University of Wisconsin, Madison*

Malawi presents a fascinating case study for global media flows: a country full of American product, with much of it there because of an informal economy, and, conversely, little of it there because of any effort on Hollywood's part to develop Malawi as a market. This article therefore draws from ethnographic fieldwork conducted in Malawi during the summers of 2008 and 2010 to examine the circulation of foreign film and television and to detail a form of media mobility through piracy.

As the fight between Steven Seagal and his latest assailant rages on the 17-inch television screen, the blaring speakers outside attract some passersby. They peek their heads into the small room that already holds 20 young men, and some decide to come in, paying their money, parking their bikes at the front of the room, and quickly finding a spot to sit. The owner of this establishment in Liwonde, Malawi, assures me that Seagal is a local favorite, matched only by Jean-Claude Van Damme, Sylvester Stallone, Arnold Schwarzenegger, and Wesley Snipes in popularity. Indeed, the "playbill" next to where he stands underscores the point, as the cover to the pirated DVD, held to the cardboard playbill by an elastic band, has clearly been worn down by time. This DVD was just as clearly an excellent investment. It contains not only the present movie, the 1990 *Marked for Death*, but also 13 other movies with Seagal, crammed in at a low resolution. Yet the owner bought the DVD for about two U.S. dollars two years ago in 2008, and he has been able to play it weekly since, charging about five U.S. cents to each viewer each time.

Such is the environment in which much Hollywood film is watched in Malawi, in "video shows" playing pirated material. Yet, lest one worry about Seagal's or Twentieth Century Fox's lost revenues, no original copy of *Marked for Death* nor of any other Hollywood film or television show can be bought in Malawi. American film and television abound, yet unless watched in one of the country's two cinemas or on the pan-African DStv satellite service, this film and television is watched on pirated DVDs. As such, Malawi presents a fascinating case study for global media flows, a country full of American product, yet with much of it there because of an informal economy, and, conversely, little of it there because of any effort on Hollywood's part to develop Malawi as a market. This article will draw from fieldwork conducted in Malawi during the summers of 2008 and 2010 when I was based in the Southern town of Liwonde yet conducting research in other Southern towns and cities including Blantyre, Limbe, Balaka, and Zomba. There, I interviewed or talked casually with more than 40 video store or stall owners, and I interviewed 22 video show owners and 50 patrons (though this article examines only the owners' responses). I examine this case further in the hopes of detailing a form of media mobility through piracy that while pervasive is discussed too rarely in global media studies.

## CHANNELS OF FLOW: HOW MEDIA MOVES GLOBALLY

Analyses of global media flows are commonly structured as entailing an epic battle between media multinationals and local consumers. The multinational creates media, then uses its international holdings and exploits its economy of scale advantages to distribute the media globally, and audiences from Albania to Zimbabwe are left to deal with the results. As embedded in the New World Information and Communication Order (NWICO) and ensuing UNESCO MacBride Report discussions of the 1970s and 1980s (see Thussu 2000, pp. 43–50) and as alleged by Herbert Schiller (1976) and Armand Mattelart (1983), many earlier versions of this tale attributed significant or almost complete power to the multinational producer in this equation, thereby giving birth to concerns of cultural imperialism and Americanization. Many recent accounts of global media flows have significantly nuanced this story, though, whether through noting the agency of international audiences in domesticating and repurposing Hollywood (see Katz & Liebes, 1990; Murphy & Kraidy, 2003; Sreberny-Mohammadi, 1997; Tomlinson, 1997), discussing "contra-flows" not simply originating from the West (Thussu, 2007), discussing the variable strengths and weaknesses of identity encoding in the media that moves (Gray, 2008; Iwabuchi, 2002), observing the deviousness by which cultural imperialism can work with local partners or "compradors" (Harindranath, 2003), or noting the "New International Division of Cultural Labor" whereby Hollywood can maintain power just as effectively through co-production deals and outsourcing as through obvious imperialism (Miller et al., 2005). As a result of such work, our understanding of how media move around the globe and with what effects has improved significantly. Along with this trend, more scholars have turned their attention to the markets by which Hollywood moves. Miller et al. (2005), for instance, note the bargain basement pricing of American television that ensures its free flow around the world; Timothy Havens (2000) examines the logics by which some shows or genres are sold and others are not; and Havens (2000, 2006), Steemers (2004), Straubhaar (2007), and Bielby and Harrington (2008) have all offered exacting reports on the specifics of the global media marketplace. Concurrently, if earlier work often assumed and ignored reception contexts, the growth in global ethnographies of production and reception has vastly improved our collective knowledge of what obstacles and competition international media face as they arrive in any given country.

But what of media's unofficial markets and of the ever-mushrooming informal economy in media sales? Though a survey of Hollywood's global holdings may justifiably worry many, Hollywood's marketing and sales teams are by no means responsible for all media flows around the globe. To begin, Hollywood simply does not care about some markets. Herman and McChesney note, for example, that when the *Financial Times* printed a map of MTV's expansion, the entire continent of Africa was removed and replaced by a list of European countries with MTV channels (1997, p. 65). Much is made of Rupert Murdoch and his colleagues' scramble to capture the Chinese or Indian markets so that as they grow, the power of a few companies grows with them. But beyond the wealthy nations of Europe and East Asia, the developing BRIC giants, and a few select others, Hollywood can and does regard many countries of the world as too poor to bother with. American film and television may move around the world and may still be popular in the markets that Hollywood shuns, but Hollywood does not control all of this movement. Motion Picture Association of America (MPAA) estimates on revenues lost due to piracy should be regarded skeptically, as personally interested and as strategically inflated (see Yar, 2005). However, even if we steeply discount the organization's estimate of $514 billion of lost revenues due to intellectual property theft (McDonald, 2007, p. 187), we still must realize the major force that piracy and the informal economy of Hollywood play in global media flows. China alone is estimated to produce nearly five billion pirated optical discs per year (McDonald, 2007, p. 203). Importantly, too, while MPAA talk of "lost revenues" often depicts a scenario in which pirated discs are purchased *instead of* a legitimate, fully legal product, given Hollywood's lack of interest and official involvement in numerous world markets we should expect that pirated discs may be the only available option in many cases (see Mattelart, 2009). Hollywood stars may be everywhere, in other words, but they are not necessarily there because of any sales effort on the part of MPAA members.

Global media studies is thus left with a relative gap, as too little work examines the multiple other means by which media move. As Tristan Mattelart notes, as significant as much work on transnational media movements is, "these studies deal essentially with the 'official' structures, actors and flows of the media economy, ignoring on the whole the shadowy structures, the actors in media piracy and the clandestine flows through which a large part of the distribution of cultural products in the South and the East is organized" (2009, p. 311). Global film and television piracy has received nothing like the rich academic detailing that the official media marketplace enjoys.[1] Even "piracy" is a clumsy term, not only because of its pejorative connotations that invoke "stolen" revenues in situations in which no revenue was sought, but also because it encompasses and conflates too wide a range of practices and players. The world's many unofficial and informal media markets significantly complicate how we can make sense of the business and meanings of media. After all, the frames through which we are presented any text or message become a vital part of that text or message. "American film" and "American television" are entities whose meanings and values will change depending on the venue in which they are presented. Therefore, while political economists and cultural studies scholars may argue over the relative importance of production and reception in the cultural placement of American media globally, we must not lose sight of *distribution* in these discussions and debates. It is with this in mind that I turn to Malawi, a country with next to no official Hollywood presence and yet one whose citizens regularly watch American film and television. How did Steven Seagal and *Marked for Death* get to a town in Southern Malawi, and how might this matter in our understanding of global media flows?

## AMERICAN FILM AND TELEVISION IN MALAWI

Malawi has only two cinemas (a third has questionable status at time of writing), one each for the main cities Blantyre and Lilongwe. The vast majority of Malawians have never been into

---

[1]For notable exceptions, see Athique, 2008; Klinger, 2010; Larkin, 2004; Mattelart, 2009; McDonald, 2007; Shi, 2010; Wang and Zhu, 2003; Yar, 2005.

a traditional cinema, instead watching films either on television or at video shows. The former outlet, however, is limited to a small elite. The country has had a single public broadcasting station since 1999, TVM, but programming is restricted mostly to parliamentary proceedings, soccer matches, sermons, and music videos, with no movies. Based in South Africa and launched in 1995, satellite service provider DStv can provide a television owner with up to 100 extra video channels (though sometimes as few as 17), approximately 30 of which play movies (though only a few exclusively), and also numerous audio channels. Satellite dishes have been on the rise, but most informants guessed that at most 20% of Malawians living in urban areas have satellite, with much fewer, if any, in most rural areas. At a cost of 10,000 kwacha per month (about US$67) and with a national GDP per capita of $900, satellite is unattainable to a significant majority of Malawians. The satellite audience expands somewhat through sharing, as satellite owning households will often host neighbors, but such a service is most commonly reserved for soccer matches or other special events, not for movies or American television shows. One could also go to a bar or restaurant with satellite, though these are by no means common outside of Blantyre and Lilongwe, with only a handful if that in most towns, and their public setting makes them appropriate mostly for soccer, sermons, music videos, news, and soaps, with few if any movies or television shows other than soaps on exhibition.

For many Malawians, then, movies are watched in video shows such as the one described at the top of this article. Video shows abound, with four or five in most towns. Patrons pay between 5 and 20 kwacha (3–12 US cents) to enter a small, dark room that holds anywhere from 20 people on the low end to 50 or 60 on the high end. A television, DVD player, and sound system sit at the front, and rows of benches are made of simple planks of wood over slabs of concrete or upturned buckets (see Figure 1). In all the 40 or so video shows I saw or attended, the televisions were small tubes, meaning the picture is at times hard to see. Video show etiquette was correspondingly impressive, with most patrons leaning forward low to allow those behind them to see, and rarely engaging in much chatter with one another. Video show owners have a simple board outside, onto which they affix the DVD cover of whatever is playing, and of what is scheduled for the rest of the day, usually with estimated times attached (see Figure 2). Patrons, though, can stay inside for as long as they want for a single fare, and local snack and drink sellers occasionally come through to provide food and drink to those who pay for them.

No hard and fast taboos exist against women attending video shows, though in part because Malawian women have significantly less leisure time than do men (Anglewicz et al., 2005), the rooms are overwhelmingly and often exclusively populated by men and boys. The shows are usually run by a pair of teen boys, and the age of patrons tends to range from pre-teen to 30s. Some are poor, some better off, though the country's (very small) upper class will rarely if ever be spotted in a video show.

Video show owners purchase their pirated DVDs from the same source ubiquitously available to others: the video stores and stalls that exist in almost every market, often in multiples of three or four per town (see Figure 3). The thriving market in Blantyre's neighboring suburb, Limbe, is home to 40 or so stalls. Stall owners will have walls packed with DVDs of film and TV, as well as CDs and VCDs of music (see Figure 4). The going rate for DVDs was 500 kwacha (US$3.50). DVDs, as will soon be discussed, are heavily packed at a low resolution, with often as many as 30 films on one disk or with an entire season of a television show (see Figure 5). I talked to more than 40 stall or store owners, and all claimed to sell to a diverse assortment of Malawians. The video show owners buy exclusively from the store and stall owners, richer Malawians frequented

FIGURE 1  The inside of a video show in Liwonde, Malawi (color figure available online).

FIGURE 2  The "marquee" for a video show in Rumphi, Malawi (color figure available online).

their stores, and many individuals with a television and a DVD player also relied on them for films and television shows. Perhaps the best way to describe the "average" patron is to describe the stalls that habitually surrounded video stores, some of which would sell used clothing, or batteries and repaired radios, or biscuits and soft drinks, or fresh produce. In other words, they

FIGURE 3 A video stall in Limbe, Malawi (color figure available online).

were part of the everyday environment of markets, an expected part of what any given market would offer. As Suavé notes more prominently of the estimated 300,000 people working within the pirate economy in Nigeria (cited in Mattelart, 2009, p. 319), piracy is booming business in Malawi, employing many.

Video shows and DVD stalls and stores were free of any stigma of illegality that might surround them in the West. With so few Malawians having access to any supposedly "legitimate" market, and with Hollywood and other multinationals showing no interest in developing the Malawian media market, pirated DVDs were nearly always the only physical form that movies or television took. If ever I asked a stall owner if she or he was worried about being arrested, the owner would give me a perplexed look, not understanding how his or her business might be considered illegal. I regularly saw policemen strolling by such stores—one stall in Liwonde was even set up next to a permanent police road block—so their lack of fear seemed wholly justified.

Almost all film and television in Malawi, therefore, either arrives in the country via DStv—who must purchase films and programs from the same syndication market as television stations worldwide—or via an assortment of unregulated means wholly outside Hollywood's purview. Hollywood, as such, has no direct dealings with Malawi or Malawian businessmen but for the rental prices for the nation's two movie theaters. With this, they invest no capital into advertising their products. Certainly, this latter lack is stark. No ads for movies adorn bus stops or roadside billboards; the national newspaper *The Nation* might advertise DStv as a service but advertises no specific text; very little is said about specific movies or television in the press in general, and no tradition of film or television criticism exists; radio ads never push this or that movie or show; and so the vast panoply of industry-led hype that surrounds film and television in wealthier

FIGURE 4  The DVD selection in a video store in Zomba, Malawi (color
figure available online).

nations is reduced to spot commercials on satellite television channels, and to individual video
show, stall, or store owners encouraging their own patrons to watch this or that.

The above picture still leaves us, however, with the question of how material gets to the stall
or store owners who serve as the nerve center of much of the nation's film and television consumption. As part of my research, I talked to all video stall or store owners who I could find in
Liwonde, Balaka, Zomba, Limbe, and Blantyre, and I asked all of them about the provenance of
their stock. All echoed the same story; that is, once a week or fortnight they would visit Blantyre,
where a few individuals would replenish their supply of DVDs. Only a few of the stall or store
owners took a concerted interest in exactly what DVDs they were given in Blantyre, as instead
most explained that their suppliers were in turn getting their stock from Johannesburg, and that
they had to make do with what was available. Whether as an adaptive or causative response,
most of the stall or store owners expressed considerable trust, though, in their supplier's tastes.
Indeed, with the lone exception of some stores or stalls that sold only West African film or television, most stalls or stores had fairly similar merchandise for sale, and few who I met showed
interest in specializing in any niche genre, star, or so forth. Some stall owners professed to have
favorites and claimed to demand these favorites and these alone, but such claims were often made
as bravado, with the owner's collection looking entirely similar to a competitor who claimed no
such specialization.

FIGURE 5  The back of a pirated DVD for sale in Balaka, Malawi (color
figure available online).

The owners were usually cagey about putting me in touch with their suppliers but would happily discuss the supply process. Again, the same story was often repeated: the DVDs came to Blantyre either direct from Nigeria in the case of West African film or television or from a few men from Johannesburg who would drive up to Blantyre occasionally in the case of all other film and television. The men from Johannesburg were further described as suppliers themselves for pirate networks in China. Certainly, many of the blurbs on the DVD packaging betrayed their Chinese origins, as Chinese phrases are occasionally mixed in with the poorly written English. *Lost* season one, for example, confusingly for an English reader, notes that "ABC Chi Juzi in Hawaii filming the whole story ups and downs, actors performing most vividly," and later offers that "Cenjinglaiguo and they seem to like the people their distress signals had been the release of the 16, but it seems that no one found their presence." Another DVD backcover for *Deadwood* season two expresses particular interest in the Chinese laborers in the program. Many DVD menus, moreover, are in Chinese and English, subtitles regularly come in both languages, and some covers even boast outright of being from China or are otherwise adorned with Chinese symbols (see Figure 6). Johannesburg was clearly the node through which non-West African DVDs came to Blantyre, and then outwards to half of the country,[2] but the DVDs began their lives in China.

I was surprised to hear of very few acts of ripping and burning occurring in the country itself, even though I often pressed the owners on whether some films and shows were copied locally. Local copying was common for CDs, and owners would often walk me lovingly through their locally copied versions of Dolly Parton CDs, for instance, but few DVDs were local products. Several stall owners helpfully pointed me to "a certain boy in Lilongwe" who apparently could copy anything I wanted, but it became clear that his business consisted of downloading film or television for foreigners in Malawi, not in supplying video shows or stall or store owners. When I followed up with questions as to why no Malawians bought from him, I was told that his DVDs would not work in their machines and that they did not have covers. Reading between the lines, it seems as though he burned the DVDs as video files for play in computers, not as readable by DVD players. Meanwhile, few other Malawians seemed active in ripping and burning DVDs themselves, instead simply distributing DVDs from Nigeria or from China by way of Johannesburg and Blantyre.

While I will spare the reader an exhaustive list of film and television available in the stalls, stores, and video shows, a sampling of the American offerings nevertheless illustrates the mix of dominant genres and eclectic outliers. West African soaps and action films regularly accounted for anywhere from a quarter to half of what was available in stalls and stores, with occasional stalls or stores specializing in them, and though Nollywood soaps were often playing in bars and restaurants at lunchtime, I never saw one playing or advertised as forthcoming in a video show. Occasionally one could find Bollywood films, and in the university town of Zomba I found a few Korean films, but for the most part everything else on offer was either a Chinese or Hong Kong martial arts film or American.

The American film offerings centered predominantly on action stars. Jean-Claude Van Damme, Arnold Schwarzenegger, Stephen Seagal, Wesley Snipes, Tom Cruise, Jason Stratham,

---

[2]Though some of my fieldwork was conducted in Rumphi and Mzuzu in the North, and Lilongwe and Mangochi in the center of the country, my interviews of stall and store owners was limited to my work in the South. Thus, it is possible and indeed probable that trade routes for the rest of the country differ.

FIGURE 6   The cover of a pirated DVD for sale in Limbe, Malawi (color figure available online).

Sylvester Stallone, and company were prominent in what was available, and on the packaging itself. DVDs, as noted above, regularly held multiple movies, clearly posing something of a challenge to the designer of the cover, and star-centered DVDs made the job easy. A more recent outing by the star might be depicted, with the DVD also including much of that star's back-catalog. Alternately, many DVD covers promised "Latest American Hero," "Fast Action 2009," "Best Movies of 2010," or so forth, usually again with a few recent films (most often action films) and a seemingly random mix of older action movies added on. War movies were common, as were war movie collections, and occasional franchise-centered DVDs were to be found, including James Bond collections or "Star Wars vs. Harry Potter" (with the *Spider-Man* and *Batman* films added on the same DVD for good measure).

Drama was almost entirely absent, unless the drama took place in a war setting, thereby facilitating partnership with other war movies, or unless it took place in Africa. Examples of the latter would often include *Sarafina*, *Cry Freedom*, *Tsotsi*, *Blood Diamond*, or *Invictus*, alongside the always-included comedies *The Gods Must Be Crazy I* and *II*, sometimes *African Queen*, *Zulu*, or other older films, and occasionally *Roots*, *Amistad*, or other films about the American slave trade. American romances were extremely rare, as I saw them at only two stores. Comedies were largely restricted to physical and slapstick humor, as with *Mr. Bean*, the aforementioned *Gods Must Be Crazy*, and collections of Charlie Chaplin films, or to collections of African American comedies, with the films of Tyler Perry enjoying especially wide circulation. Many stalls also owned a single DVD full of animated films, and some owned a lone horror collection.

As for television, action was again central. *24* and *Prison Break* were easily more common than any other show, with the British *Primeval* common too. *CSI* and *CSI: Miami* were everywhere in 2008, but nowhere to be seen when I returned in 2010. Instead, *Lost* was now enjoying wide circulation, as was *Desperate Housewives*. Most seasons of the above shows were available, albeit rarely at the same stall or store, but a sign of the eclectic availability of American television could be found in how few of the other available shows offered a full season range. Thus, for instance, *Deadwood* season two was ubiquitous, yet seasons one and three were nowhere to be found. Oddly, season three of *Monk* was for sale at a few stalls (though one owner insisted to me that it was a bad show and that I would not like it), as were seasons four of *One Tree Hill* and *Xena: Warrior Princess* and seasons two of *The Wire* and *The Unit*. Indeed, it was in asking stall or store owners why they only had one season of a show that I regularly heard them explain that they simply sold what they were given. Even when I expressed interest in purchasing future seasons, the same stall owners who would eagerly seek out music for me and provide it in a future visit were clear, if apologetic, in insisting that they could not produce video on request.

## PIRATE SHIPS ON THE GLOBAL MEDIA FLOWS

At first glance, the above picture may suggest business as usual for global media flows—a non-American country saturated by American media. However, Malawi is, in fact, quite exceptional in terms of much of the printed work on global media for two key reasons.

First, Malawi has next to no domestic film or television production. When asked if they had seen a Malawian film, most informants laughed at the concept, and/or told me about a string of five low-budget action films with the same star.[3] Nobody had heard of any other Malawian film.[4] Meanwhile, most of TVM's programming consists of filming material already in progress. Thus, foreign film and television compete almost entirely with themselves, not with local production. Whereas much discussion of global media flows and contra-flows, and especially of cultural imperialism, has focused on countries with developed production cores that are threatened by Hollywood, Malawi is no India, China, Japan, or Brazil. This situation raises a barrage of questions that it is beyond the scope of this article to answer. How might entire media, in this case, film and television, be conceived of differently in a context in which they are only foreign? How are they placed culturally and relative to other media, such as music or journalism, which do offer local variants? Might theories of media imports operating at a "cultural discount" need to be transformed when there is no "full price" local competition? Or, how might Hollywood, Nollywood, Chinese/Hong Kong film, and pan-African television programming be body-blocking the development of a local production core? Such questions point to a need for ethnographies of reception and production (or even of *would-be* production) that ask different questions and that attend to different issues than global media studies has often raised.

Second, though, Malawi provides a fascinating case study in terms of how media are distributed and of the dynamics of media supply and demand. With very few exceptions, none of the film or television in Malawi was produced with a Malawian audience in mind. Even DStv, which offers channels catering to different language groups across the continent, caters to Malawi in no way. While, as Moradewun Adejunmobi notes in this special issue, DStv offers AfricaMagic Yoruba and AfricaMagic Hausa, thereby targeting specific ethnic-linguistic groups within Nigeria, there is no AfricaMagic Chichewa, Yao, or Tambuka. Malawi is a nation doubly marginalized by media multinationals. Africa as a whole has often been ignored by many of the corporations that otherwise boast of their global satellite footprints, and Malawi is ignored even within Africa. A nation of 14.8 million people with a precipitously low GDP, Malawi is of no interest to media multinationals.

Film piracy in particular is thus a wholly different creature in Malawi. The MPAA frequently decries lost revenues due to piracy, always offering phenomenally high estimates of the dollar loss. Some critics have fairly countered not only that piracy may be the price of doing business in various markets but also that pirated films may be instrumental in creating an audience for Hollywood (see Miller et al., 2005, p. 215). Boyd et al. (1989, p. 35), Miller et al. (2005), Mattelart (2009), and Klinger (2010) have even shown that piracy can prove important in breaking through censorship walls and networks of state control, creating further demand for Hollywood where none may have otherwise existed or been allowed. Even in the absence of restrictive censorship policies or tight control of cultural imports, the MPAA has never shown any signs of caring about Malawi in the first place. Thus, when a video show owner in Balaka plays *Mission Impossible 3* to a room full of 40 young men, neither J. J. Abrams, Tom Cruise, nor United International ever tried to sell the film "legitimately" to this audience, making it hard to argue that they have lost any revenue. Similarly, no business attempts to sell nonpirated copies

---

[3]Unfortunately, nobody could provide copies of these films to me, and most insisted that I would not want to watch them anyway, often expressing embarrassment at their poor quality and/or mocking them mercilessly. Moreover, many who were aware of them had not actually seen them, only heard of them.

[4]A very small number of films have been made in Malawi, but these tend to be made available internationally in film festivals, and none save the low budget action films were known to any of my respondents.

of Hollywood films in Malawi, and so the pervasive market in stalls and stores for pirated fare is not a "black market" competitor—it is the only market. The densely laden rhetoric of "piracy" is unhelpful to an understanding of Malawian media distribution, to the point that we might be better to avoid the term altogether. Just as we might hesitate to call those who take supplies from an abandoned port "pirates," Malawi's video show, stall, and store owners hardly qualify as pirates in the absence of a "legitimate" rival contesting their sales.

The metaphor of an abandoned port might help direct us to another reality with the Malawian media picture—Malawians had little or no say in what materials made it to Malawi. This is not a case of strategic raids being conducted on specific Hollywood media providers, genres, or so forth; rather, Malawi's store and stall owners are left with whatever the Chinese pirates decided to copy and send to Johannesburg, and in turn with what their South African counterparts decided to send to Blantyre. Clearly, the Chinese pirates work with some operating logics. Star-driven action films, war movies, and slapstick, physical comedies are all especially common, suggesting that the Chinese pirates place a premium on them selling internationally and across linguistic barriers. Collections of movies set in Africa were also common, as were collections of any movies with a predominantly Black cast; given that these often lacked Chinese subtitles or covers, moreover, we see evidence that Chinese pirates thought these would sell especially and only in Africa. However, with no direct trade between these pirates and the Malawians who sell the material, and with little if any mechanism for communicating Malawian demand and desires back to the Chinese pirates, Malawi is left with no real choice about what film or television arrives there, nor do its interests seem to factor into decision making about what to copy except at the broadest and crudest of levels (i.e., that Africans as a whole might like material with Black actors).

As an unintended market for Hollywood, Malawi is also home to no real advertising for film or television. Without the newest film or show being touted as bigger and better, we therefore see an interesting shift in the temporality of media flows. Rather than be awash with a continuing current of new product, Malawian video stalls and stores have as much room for and do as much business selling Chaplin, Schwarzenegger, and Stallone films and the likes of *African Queen* and *Cry Freedom* as they do for anything newer. The owners have little incentive to sell only new texts either. Thus, upon asking for recommendations, I was just as often directed to a collection of older Bruce Lee or Steven Seagal films as to recent Hollywood blockbusters. If anything, older fare sold better, in part because of its familiarity and hence perceived reliability. Video show exhibition choices showed a marked trend towards showing action films from the 1980s and early 1990s, and whereas Van Damme, Stallone, Schwarzenegger, and Seagal were widely known and recognized by the owners and patrons to whom I talked, characters such as Batman and Spider-Man or more recent stars such as Russell Crowe or Brad Pitt were considerably less known.

All of the above challenges how we analyze media flows in a country such as Malawi. If one asks after the who, what, why, when, where, and how of media mobility and circulation in many other contexts, Hollywood seems the natural answer to all questions—Hollywood is seen as determining what enters a country, when it enters, and how it enters. Here these questions must be asked anew. The content entering Malawi is a somewhat random assortment of material, decided upon in the first instance by Chinese pirates, not Hollywood executives, and in the second instance by contacts for those pirates in Johannesburg. Thus, Hollywood may be prevalent in Malawi, but it has come by way of China, Johannesburg, and then Blantyre. The material also comes at differing speeds—sometimes a stall owner would return from Blantyre with *The Dark Knight*, *Hurt Locker*, or something reasonably recent, but he would just as often return with "new" DVDs containing 30-year-old films or season one of *24*. DStv, meanwhile, would similarly broadcast a mix of recent American shows and older films.

With few exceptions in Malawi, we see a stratification of media processes by country and level of organization. A significant proportion of film and television in the country has been produced by media multinationals based in the United States, but it has been distributed by a mixture of the South African based DStv and the informal economy of pirate networks that stretch outwards from Blantyre to Johannesburg, China, and presumably the United States where many films and television are originally copied. In the case of American films and television, these are thus filtered by way of numerous intermediaries of varying distances away from the directives of Hollywood and/or the U.S. State Department. While media flows are often imagined to move fairly directly from the producing country to the receiving country, multiple other agents direct the process here, exerting pressure to move Hollywood's materials when none is present from the MPAA or the major television companies themselves, and governed by radically different business norms and practices, if not also cultural intentions and motivations.

Any analysis of media flows in Malawi subsequently requires a careful analysis of the ways in which these intermediaries act as filters. Especially if we are to examine theories of cultural imperialism on influence, for instance, the variously conspicuous or inconspicuous presence of these intermediaries proves important. When media has come to Malawi from the United States by way of China and South Africa, it may have picked up or lost certain frames and cultural baggage along the way. If, as Koichi Iwabuchi (2002) notes, media may have a "cultural odor," we need to ask what media "smells" like after its long, circuitous route to Malawi. After all, not only do DStv and pirate networks play a role in moving media to and around Malawi, but they are also *seen* to be doing so. DStv is well known to be a product of South Africa, and when Malawian cultural relationships with South Africa are conflicted and at times highly contentious, we would be foolish not to expect DStv's "South Africanness" to be seen to color films or television shows that arrive in Malawi. Pirated DVDs, too, announce their Chinese provenance with Chinese symbols on the packaging and in menus, requiring us once more to inquire into the complicating factor that China plays in any American-Malawian media movement. Meanwhile, of course, the ubiquity of pirated foreign content available at low cost is likely stifling any potential development of Malawian film or television production more successfully and completely than the official presence of Hollywood ever could, thereby further drawing our attention to how networks of distribution within informal economies affect the possibilities of production within legal, "legitimate" economies.

Indeed, this article could be seen to represent the frustration of a partly failed project: I went to Malawi in part to understand how foreign media moved around the country and what it meant, and soon found that many of the answers lay in Johannesburg and in China. The project, however, also illustrates the centrality of *distribution* to media mobility. While discussions of cultural imperialism and global media flows have often either begun in medias res, with the media already in the country in question and with little interest in how it got there, or have assumed Hollywood's active, purposeful, and continuing role in flooding the country in question with content, the case of foreign media in Malawi calls for greater attention to be paid to the various intermediaries and means by which media and culture "flow" across the globe. Global media flows have more often been studied with political economic analyses of production and policy and/or with ethnographies of reception, but Malawi shows the need for more ethnographies of distribution.

# REFERENCES

Adejunmobi, M. (this issue). Nollywood, globalization, and regional media corporations in Africa. *Popular Communication, 9*(2), 67–78.

Anglewicz, P., Bignami-Van Assche, S., Fleming, P., Van Assche, A., & van de Ruit, C. (2005). *The impact of HIV/AIDS on intra-household time allocation in rural Malawi.* Philadelphia, PA: University of Pennsylvania Population Studies Center Working Paper.

Athique, A. (2008). The global dynamics of Indian media piracy: Export markets, playback media and the informal economy. *Media, Culture and Society, 30*(5), 699–717.

Bielby, D. D., & Harrington, C. L. (2008). *Global TV: Exporting television and culture in the world market.* New York, NY: New York University Press.

Boyd, D. A., Straubhaar, J. D., & Lent, J. A. (1989). *Videocassette recorders in the Third World.* White Plains, NY: Longman.

Gray, J. (2008). Imagining America: *The Simpsons* go global. *Popular Communication, 5*(2), 129–148.

Harindranath, R. (2003). Reviving "cultural imperialism": International audiences, global capitalism, and the transnational elite. In L. Parks & S. Kumar (Eds.), *Planet TV: A global television reader* (pp. 155–168). New York, NY: NYU Press.

Herman, E. S., & McChesney, R. W. (1997). *The global media: The new missionaries of global capitalism.* Washington, DC: Cassell.

Havens, T. (2000). "The biggest show in the world": Race and the global popularity of *The Cosby Show. Media, Culture and Society, 22*(4), 371–391.

Havens, T. (2006). *Global television marketplace.* London, England: British Film Institute.

Iwabuchi, K. (2002). *Recentering globalization: Popular culture and Japanese transnationalism.* Durham, NC: Duke University Press.

Katz, E., & Liebes, T. (1990). *The export of meaning: Cross-cultural readings of Dallas.* New York, NY: Oxford University Press.

Klinger, B. (2010). Contraband cinema: Piracy, *Titanic,* and Central Asia. *Cinema Journal, 49*(2), 106–124.

Larkin, B. (2004). Degraded images, distorted sounds: Nigerian video and the infrastructures of piracy. *Public Culture, 16*(2), 289–314.

Mattelart, A. (1983). *Transnationals and Third World: The struggle for culture.* South Hadley, MA: Bergin & Garvey.

Mattelart, T. (2009). Audio-visual piracy: Towards a study of the underground networks of cultural globalization. *Global Media and Communication, 5*(3), 308–326.

McDonald, P. (2007). *Video and DVD industries.* London, England: British Film Institute.

Miller, T., Govil, N., McMurria, J., Maxwell, R., & Wang, T. (2005). *Global Hollywood 2.* London, England: British Film Institute.

Murphy, P. D., & Kraidy, M. M. (Eds.). (2003). *Global media studies: Ethnographic perspectives.* New York, NY: Routledge.

Schiller, H. (1976). *Communication and cultural domination.* Armonk, NY: M. E. Sharpe.

Shi, Yu. (2010). Product placement and digital piracy: How young Chinese viewers react to the unconventional method of corporate cultural globalization. *Communication, Culture and Critique, 3*(3), 435–463.

Sreberny-Mohammadi, A. (1997). The many faces of imperialism. In P. Golding & P. Harris (Eds.), *Beyond cultural imperialism* (pp. 48–68). Thousand Oaks, CA: Sage.

Steemers, J. (2004). *Selling television: British television in the global media marketplace.* London, England: British Film Institute.

Straubhaar, J. D. (2007). *World television: From global to local.* Thousand Oaks, CA: Sage.

Thussu, D. K. (2000). *International communication: Continuity and change.* London, England: Arnold.

Thussu, D. K. (Ed.). (2007). *Media on the move: Global flow and contra-flow.* New York, NY: Routledge.

Tomlinson, J. (1997). Cultural globalization and cultural imperialism. In A. Mohammadi (Ed.), *International communication and globalization* (pp. 170–190). Thousand Oaks, CA: Sage.

Wang, S., & Zhu, J. J. H. (2003). Mapping film piracy in China. *Theory, Culture and Society, 20*(4), 97–125.

Yar, M. (2005). The global "epidemic" of movie "piracy": Crime-wave or social construction? *Media, Culture and Society, 27*(5), 677–696.

# "Honorable Piracy" and Chile's Digital Transition

Jennifer Ashley

*George Mason University*

This article examines debates around Chile's digital television transition in order to trace the socio-historical relation between piracy and social change. During the military dictatorship (1973–1990), media activists used what they called "honorable piracy" for counter-communication efforts aimed at restoring democracy. Following the return to democracy, community television participants have rationalized their unauthorized transmission of alternative programming to low-income sectors using a similar logic of honorable piracy. For these community television participants, the digital transition represented the possibility of redefining democratic access to the public sphere and attaining legal recognition. Through an analysis of citizen activism around the move from analog to digital television, this article argues that discussion of piracy emerges as an expression of conflicting notions of the definition, use, and distribution of public resources.

In October 2009, a group of Chilean community television station participants met in the beach town of Pichilemu to organize around the upcoming digital television legislation. One of the organizers of the meeting was Polo Lillo, founding member of Chile's oldest community television station, Señal 3- La Victoria. A statement he made to the group set the tone for the meeting: "We're pirate televisions! Clandestine in democracy! Clandestine television! How is that possible? That's what hurts." Polo's frustration was due to the fact that Señal 3, like all of the community television stations in Chile, operated outside a legal framework. For the community television activists present at this meeting, digital television transition represented the possibility of legal recognition and a more profound democratization of Chile's media system.

Polo's choice of the word pirate, and the disgust he expressed when he used it, provides an entryway into exploring the complex relation between citizens' media and the Chilean state. Chilean community television's unauthorized transmission emerges from a long history of piracy-related activist practices aimed at democracy-building and social change. The urgency that marked Polo's intervention in this particular moment was linked to the parallel that he and other community television participants drew between the digital transition and the democratic transition that had occurred in 1990. Framed differently, the citizens' movement around Chile's digital television legislation approached the digital transition as a moment of socio-political, as well as technological, change. The activism of Chilean community television participants around the digital transition provides empirical evidence of the multiple subject positions that citizens' media projects adopt in response to "pirate" practices. Although Chilean community television activists supported the liberatory potential of what Castells and Cardoso (2012) have called "piracy cultures" in other instances, being denominated "pirate" for unauthorized transmission indexed for the participants at this meeting social stasis, rather than social change. That is to say, it signaled the continued postponement by the state of their legitimate participation within a democratic public sphere.

In this article, I focus on Chile's digital transition as a moment that makes visible conflicting ideas of democratic order. At the time of this meeting of the Network of Community Television Stations (RTP), a digital television bill had been introduced into Congress that was, by these activists' standards, far inferior to similar laws generated in other Latin American countries. For the community television participants gathered in Pichilemu, the digital television transition had democratizing potential. Transition from analog to digital technology allowed for greater bandwidth efficiency and, therefore, the possibility of an increased number of channels.[1] The digital transition for them was thus an invitation to each country to determine whether or not to redistribute the electromagnetic spectrum among a greater number of participants. Community television activists (such as those from Señal 3- La Victoria and Canal 3-Pichilemu) argued that the electromagnetic spectrum was a publicly shared resource, and that as citizens they had a right to access it and to determine its distribution. Aligning with other likeminded organizations, they demanded that the digital television legislation stipulate that the state would reserve space in the spectrum for educational, cultural, and community programming, as well as independent production.[2]

My analysis of the activism of Chilean community television participants around the digital transition draws from discussion of "piracy cultures" (Castells & Cardoso, 2012), as well as the role of political subjectivity in shaping responses to piracy (Dent, 2012a, 2012b; Skinner, 2012). Attention to piracy in the vernacular, I suggest, demonstrates the importance of socio-cultural context in producing conflicting definitions of democratic access. In what follows, I focus on three moments in Chile's evolving conversation around piracy and the potential for social change. The first considers the significance of "honorable piracy" in the restoration of the Chilean democratic state. The second outlines the exercise of "open secret piracy" following the return to democracy, and the third focuses on the potential role of the digital transition in the redefinition of a democratic commons. Central to my discussion is a recognition of how debates around piracy and the commons reveal that transitions, both political and technological, are never finished stories, but rather ongoing reckonings with past and present debates regarding the use and distribution of publically shared resources.


## METHODOLOGY

This article emerges from long-term ethnographic fieldwork in the community television station of Señal 3 - La Victoria located in Santiago, Chile. Ethnography, as Ginsburg, Abu-Lughod, and Larkin (2002) note, is uniquely suited to exploring "how media are embedded in people's quotidian lives but also how consumers and producers are themselves imbricated in discursive

---

[1] See Galperin (2006) for a discussion of the greater bandwidth efficiency of digital television.
[2] See Mesa de Ciudadanía y TV Digital (n.d.b).

universes, political situations, economic circumstances, national settings, historical moments, and transnational flows to name only a few relevant contexts" (p. 2). Seeking to understand the digital television transition within Chile's particular social, political, and historical processes, this article draws on research trips of one- to three-month periods in 2006, 2007, 2010, 2011, 2012, and 2013, and 12 months in 2008–2009. During these research periods, I lived in the neighborhood of La Victoria and was actively engaged in the daily operations of Señal 3. Participant observation included accompanying station members in the filming, editing, and transmission of content, as well as meeting with other community television representatives, governmental representatives, and civil society organizations. As Señal 3 began to mobilize along with other community television stations in preparation for the digital television transition, I often supported their efforts by transcribing the meetings of the RTP, and working with other network members to synthesize these statements into documents that they circulated within the network and to related nongovernmental organizations (NGOs) and state actors.

My participant observation in the discussion among community television participants regarding the digital television legislation spanned three presidential periods. The Chilean digital television bill was first introduced to Congress in 2008 during Michelle Bachelet's center-left government (2006–2010). Despite Bachelet's popularity, Chilean presidents are not permitted to serve two consecutive terms, and the candidate of the center-left coalition for the 2009–2010 presidential elections did not garner sufficient public support. Debate around the digital television legislation thus continued under the right-wing government of Sebastián Piñera (2010–2014). Michelle Bachelet returned to office in 2014, and the law will go into effect during this second term of her government (2014–2018). Examining the digital television transition over these three presidential periods allows for a consideration of the relation between the state and citizens' media that goes beyond the technocratic strategy of one particular government or party.

## PIRACY CULTURES AND POLITICAL SUBJECTIVITY

Despite a surge in academic attention during the last several years, anxiety around piracy can be traced back to the 15th century book trade (Balázs, 2011; Heller-Roazen, 2009; Johns, 2009). Renewed interest in piracy accompanies advances in digital technologies that have facilitated the reproduction of cultural goods and the sharing of information, putting into question producers' control over circulation processes (Castells & Cardoso, 2012; Karaganis, 2011; Lessig, 2001, 2004). Scholars have signaled the relation between pirate practices and ideas of democracy (Lessig, 2004; Poster, 2007), as well as their relation to the tensions and contradictions associated with neoliberal capitalism (Dawdy, 2011). As Dent notes, "one of the primary reasons that piracy is simultaneously au courant and passé is that it seems to have arisen at moments when boundaries have not been quite clear, and those moments abound" (2012b, p. 661). The figure of the pirate comes to embody a wide range of practices in quite varied contexts. It is, in part, the struggle to give clarity to these situations of ambiguity that has prompted recent attempts to determine what, if anything, defines "pirate culture" (Andersson Schwarz, 2012; Dawdy & Bonni, 2012; Mylonas, 2012; Spilker, 2012). In their editorial introduction to a collection on "piracy cultures," Manuel Castells and Gustavo Cardoso argue that "when a significant proportion of the population is building its mediation through alternative channels of obtaining content, such behavior should be studied in order to deepen our knowledge of media cultures" (2012, p. 826). In this article, I draw on these discussions to emphasize how the significance of pirate practices shifts in relation to socio-historical context.

Both Dent (2012a) and Skinner (2012) use subjectivity as a theoretical lens to address the particularities of socio-historical context in shaping experiences of piracy. In his ethnography of music piracy in Brazil, Dent (2012b), for example, considers how individuals adopt seemingly paradoxical subject positions in relation to the "legitimacy" of anti-piracy discourses in one context and their everyday practices of piracy in another. He suggests that Brazil's unique experience of neoliberalism produces these two subject positions. Skinner, for his part, approaches Malian artists' concerns with piracy as a crisis of political subjectivity, which he defines as "a civic position from which claims to and arguments for secure lifeworlds and sustainable livelihoods may be expressed to reflect a community's interest in 'good'—accountable and beneficent—governance" (2012, p. 725). In my account of Chilean community television activism, I similarly draw attention to multiple subject positions in response to piracy, as well as their link to expressions of political and economic inequality.

According to Dent, "calling someone a pirate is fighting talk," whereas "declaring oneself to be a pirate is a defiant gesture directed at a powerful institution perceived to be oblivious to the greater good" (2012b, p. 662). Polo's statement at the meeting of community television activists in Pichilemu was, in a way, a combination of those two subject positions. On the one hand, he was attempting to incite the other community television participants into action by emphasizing their outsider position in relation to the democratic state that they had contributed to restoring following the end of the dictatorship in 1990. On the other, he was critiquing the legitimacy of the Chilean state's management of a democratic commons. Polo's concern did not emerge from fear of possible legal repercussions, but rather from a desire for recognition of the legitimacy of his political project. In their exploration of pirate culture, Dawdy and Bonni (2012) conclude that the figure of the pirate seems to emerge at moments when the experience of inequality has reached a crisis point. Their work suggests that the appearance of piracy signals the potential for change (p. 696). In what follows, I explore this potentiality through an analysis of the fraught relation of Chilean community television to piracy, the socio-historical construction of notions of plunder and the commons, and the role of the digital television transition in providing a context for re-evaluating democratic access to public space.

## HONORABLE PIRACY, CHILEAN DEMOCRACY, AND COMMUNITY TELEVISION

Chilean community television emerged in the late 1990s in the Población La Victoria.[3] One of Chile's most emblematic leftist neighborhoods, La Victoria was founded in 1957 through a land takeover organized by the Communist and Socialist parties. In 1970, neighborhood residents fought to elect socialist President Salvador Allende. After only three years, however, Allende was overthrown by a US-backed military coup led by Augusto Pinochet. During the 17 years of dictatorship that followed (1973–1990), La Victoria was a center of resistance (and repression). "Pirate" media became a central component of the resistance efforts of activists in La

---

[3]"Población" comes from "población callampa," or "mushroom population," and refers to low-income neighborhoods, many of which were formed through land takeovers and have long histories of political organization.

Victoria during this time period. Accessing clandestine copies of audiovisual material of protests and detentions through their sociopolitical networks, they organized public screenings to provide neighbors with news censored by the military regime. During the late 1980s, they also drew on a series of publications printed by the Chilean NGO ECO entitled *Honorable Pirates (Piratas Honradas)* for their counter communication efforts.[4] In this series of publications, ECO compiled examples of cartoons and other drawings of Latin American artists and encouraged those who wanted to design posters, pamphlets, and other sorts of small media opposing the dictatorship to copy the models provided in order to communicate their message. For activists, using the symbols elaborated by the artists allowed them to produce material more quickly and improve reception of their messages. For the artists, the value lay in the possibility of having their work cited widely, and that work becoming an index of the political ideas that they, too, shared. Copying the work of others, in this case, was considered "honorable" because it was done not for individual economic benefit, but rather for the collective political good. In this way, piracy for these Chilean activists has a specific socio-historical resonance with ties to media democratization that emerge well before the digital transition.

Shortly following the return to democratic elections in 1990, European NGOs financed "popular video" projects in La Victoria to support media pluralism and provide low-income residents with additional training in audiovisual skills.[5] Through one of these projects, residents of La Victoria accessed a television transmitter. Little by little, they gathered funds to purchase more equipment, and in 1997 they formed Chile's first community television station, which would eventually become known as "Señal 3 – La Victoria." Señal 3 participants were largely self-taught media makers working with do-it-yourself (DIY) infrastructure. They financed their project by asking for donations in the weekend fruit and vegetable markets, selling antennae that they manufactured, and occasionally receiving donations from likeminded groups in Europe. Purchasing editing software was cost-prohibitive, so these community media makers relied on pirated software to generate videos on political or cultural happenings. In addition to a few shows produced by neighborhood residents, the programming of Señal 3 included political documentaries, soccer games, and the programming of the Venezuelan-initiated pan-regional network, Telesur. For station members, the act of copying a documentary or using one cable subscription to transmit soccer games or Telesur to an entire neighborhood (that would otherwise not have the financial means to gain access to it) was a form of "honorable piracy" because it followed a logic of democratizing access to information.

In 2002, members of Señal 3 participated in a forum in Santiago on alternative media where they met Chilean exiles living in Europe committed to supporting popular communication projects. Through these contacts, they accessed a second television transmitter, which they began to lend for periods of six months to community organizations in various parts of the country. Through this system, Señal 3- La Victoria contributed to establishing more than a dozen community television stations throughout Chile, including Canal 3 Pichilemu. Although it is difficult to specify the number of community television stations operating in Chile at any one time given the absence of an official registry and the challenges that the stations face in sustaining transmission

---

[4]The first volume was printed in January 1986, the second in January 1987, and the third in July 1990 (following the return to democracy in March 1990). See Red de Prensa Popular (1986).

[5]These projects were modeled after the ideas of the popular education movement influenced by the critical pedagogy model of Brazilian educator Paulo Freire (1921–1997).

over time, representatives of the RTP estimate that between 2008 and 2014 the number of stations in operation at any one time has ranged from 15 to 25. These stations have come together for fundraising events, technical workshops, and strategic meetings to plan for the digital television legislation.

## THE ANALOG POLITICS OF OPEN SECRET PIRACY

Although Señal 3 participants have transmitted without a license since 1997, this does not mean that they transmit clandestinely. Their broadcasting—and even their unauthorized retransmission of the signal of a cable provider to the entire neighborhood—has been what would be called in Chile, a "*secreto a voces,*" or an open secret. According to neighborhood lore, representatives from the cable company would occasionally arrive in La Victoria to inspect the connection, but when they asked for the location of Señal 3, residents would point them in the wrong direction. (A quick internet search would, however, produce the correct address.) Chilean national media have done numerous feature stories on the station, and after the first few years of operation, station members stopped making an effort to hide their activities. When Señal 3 was faced with eviction unless they could raise the approximately US$16,000 needed to buy the house where the station was located, the then state-sponsored newspaper, *La Nación,* ran a story that sought to help the community media makers with their fundraising efforts (Rozas, 2008). During the analog era, open secret piracy was a way for the Chilean state to defer, but not refuse, demands for greater media democratization.

The position of Chilean community television outside a legal framework meant that they did not have access to funding through the state's Ministry of Transport and Telecommunications. However, station members have managed to access small funds for specific projects through other state agencies. The activists' meeting in Pichilemu in October 2009, for example, was made possible in part because Canal 3-Pichilemu and Señal 3-La Victoria had successfully applied for funding through the Chilean government's Division of Social Organization (DOS), enabling them to cover travel and lodging for the group of approximately 30 activists. Although the digital transition threatened to make community television's precarious position vis-à-vis the law a more pressing practical problem, Polo's concern at the meeting in Pichilemu was more closely linked to the symbolic significance of their pirate characterization. The digital television transition was the moment for the state to recognize the existence of community television. For activists such as those at Señal 3–La Victoria and Canal 3–Pichilemu, it was their opportunity to redefine democratic access to the public sphere.

Polo illustrated his critique of the state's "open secret policy" in dealing with community television by recounting to the group gathered in Pichilemu a conversation that occurred during a meeting with representatives of Bachelet's center-left government. "A legal representative from the Ministry arrived at that meeting," Polo explained. "He said, 'Don't worry, we're going to turn a blind eye to you (*hacerles la vista gorda*).'" By this, the legal representative meant that the government would not persecute them, nor confiscate their equipment. In other words, they were willing to keep the unauthorized transmission of the community television stations an open secret. Polo continued, "We said, 'Thanks very much, but we don't *need* you to turn a blind eye to us.'" He paused for effect, and then continued, "The guy said, 'The last station that we are going to close is Señal 3 of La Victoria because a lot of people inside the Ministry think just like you do.'"

Polo shared this exchange with the community television participants in order to stress that the ability of community television stations to transmit was their democratic right. Open secret piracy was, for Polo, the denial of the legitimacy of their participation in the system of governance that they had fought to put into place. The legal representative had offered paternalistic protection outside of the law by suggesting a political affinity between the Ministry and the left-leaning station of La Victoria. Polo, however, was not interested in a pledge of continued exceptionalism, but rather legal recognition as a path toward full democratic participation.

Although analog politics permitted this ambiguous relation between community television and the state, activists argued that this would no longer be tenable after the transition. Digital technology provided greater economic, technical, and legal barriers to DIY community media operators than did analog technology. In order to claim their place as stakeholders in the repartitioning of the spectrum that would accompany the digital transition, Señal 3, as well as the country's other community television stations, joined together in 2009 with more than 20 other organizations to form the *Mesa de Ciudadanía TV Digital* (which I will refer to as the "citizens' movement"). In addition to community media organizations, the citizens' movement was made up of likeminded NGOs, artist unions, and associations of independent media producers.[6] Despite expectations of a sharper digital politics to accompany digital technology, all involved soon found that ambiguities of use and distribution were not as neatly resolved as they had anticipated.

## PLUNDER AND THE DIGITAL COMMONS

By 2012, a version of what would be Chile's digital television law was circulating in the country's Congress. In a forum organized by the citizens' movement in response to the legislation, María Pía Matta, President of the World Association of Community Radios (AMARC), contrasted the Chilean legislation with the efforts by the Brazilian government to develop a public television system. "In Chile," she argued, "The media are conceived uniquely and exclusively as private . . . the notion of public—because we are using a frequency that belongs to all of us—does not exist. [In Chile] the man who has the frequency thinks that he can take it home with him." The other members of the forum laughed wryly. She continued, "And then his son will inherit it from him, and then his grandson will inherit it from him. That is Chile."[7]

With her statement, Matta shifted discussion of legitimacy from pirate media to a pirate state. For citizens' media activists, the dictatorship was an illegitimate state that had put into place neoliberal communication reforms that had allowed a wealthy few to plunder the resources of the public.[8] In contrast, the community media activists, and the other citizens' organizations that banded together with them, started with the premise that the electromagnetic spectrum was a "scarce public good belonging to all Chileans, consecrated as common patrimony of humanity."[9]

---

[6] For a full list of participants, see Mesa de Ciudadanía y TV Digital (n.d.b).

[7] See "Debate TV Pública" (2012).

[8] For a discussion of neoliberal reforms to Chile's communication system put in place during the military dictatorship, see Bresnahan (2003) and Tironi and Sunkel (2001).

[9] See Mesa de la Ciudadanía y TV Digital (2010). The Mesa is a citizens' interest group composed not only of the RTP, but also NGOs, such as the Media Observatory Fucatel. Using the language of a "public good" in relation to the bandwidth, however, was in the RTP's conversations from the beginning.

They framed their discussions with the Chilean state regarding the legislation as a debate over "the commons." Hardt and Negri define this concept in the following way:

> By "the common" we mean, first of all, the common wealth of the material world—the air, the water, the fruits of the soil, and all nature's bounty—which in classic European political texts is often claimed to be the inheritance of humanity as a whole, to be shared together. We consider the common also and more significantly those results of social production that are necessary for social interaction and further production, such as knowledges, languages, codes, information, affects, and so forth. (2009, p. viii)

However, as Hess and Ostrom note, digital technology has enabled the harnessing of this common wealth of public goods, altering the terms of access. They write:

> This ability to capture the previously uncapturable creates a fundamental change in the nature of the resource, with the resource being converted from a nonrivalrous, nonexclusionary public good into a common-pool resource that needs to be managed, monitored, and protected, to ensure sustainability and preservation. (2006, p. 10)

It is this concept of a common-pool resource that became a source of contention between the citizens' media movement and the Chilean state. For participants in the citizens' movement, the electromagnetic spectrum was very closely associated with the democratic public sphere that they had fought to regain with the end of the dictatorship. Therefore, they insisted upon their right to participate in the use, management, and protection of this resource.

One of the first public collective actions of the citizens' movement around digital television reflects this sense of ownership of the electromagnetic spectrum. In a letter to President Michelle Bachelet regarding the legislation in May 2009 they self-define as "alternative media to those validated by the prevailing neoliberal system," and continue by arguing for their right to access the spectrum and to participate in the creation of the law that would govern them.[10] By 2010, the citizens' media movement had elaborated a proposal, which addressed (among other things) the legal recognition of existing community television stations, the definition of the boundaries of what could be considered community television, the reservation of 40% of the spectrum for "educational, cultural, and community television," and the prevention of the economic concentration of the spectrum.[11] In the years that followed, they worked to educate the public, as well as politicians, on the significance of these reforms to the deepening of Chile's democracy.

In 2013, after five long years of debate, the Chilean Congress passed the Digital Television Legislation. The legislation was not one of the binaries expected of the digital era (i.e., included/excluded, resolved/unresolved, etc.) but rather a continuous spectrum of ambiguities (e.g., how to distribute it, how to measure it). Activists and academics alike critiqued the resulting law as insufficient, noting in particular that it failed to address the concerns of community television participants. One of the primary points of contention was the stipulation in the law that 40% of the electromagnetic spectrum would be reserved for "regional, local, and community channels."[12] Participants in the citizens' media movement argued that grouping together those three types of stations was problematic given that regional and local stations were commercial,

---

[10] The letter was also published in the Chilean online newspaper, *El Ciudadano*. See "Red de Televisiones Populares" (2009).

[11] For the full proposal, see Mesa de Ciudadanía y TV Digital (n.d.a).

[12] See Gobierno de Chile (2013).

whereas community channels were not. Communications scholars, such as Chiara Sáez Baeza (2013a), pointed to further aspects of ambiguity in this percentage, noting that the Subsecretary of Communications (SUBTEL) had made no announcement regarding the distribution plan of the spectrum, making it unclear how many channels would even exist following digitalization. Saéz also noted that funds were not reserved to finance the infrastructure or equipment necessary for the migration of community television stations to digital television.[13] The Chilean Media Observatory, Fucatel, similarly noted that the law did not "meet the expectations" of either the national citizens' movement (of which it formed part) or international organizations supporting media democratizations, such as UNESCO. Like Sáez, they critiqued its failure to address issues related to access for indigenous groups or the recognition of the already existing community television stations.[14]

Citizens' media activists were not the only ones, however, to accuse of plunder. Right-wing president and former owner of one of Chile's television channels, Sebastián Piñera, controversially vetoed the bill at the end of his presidential term in an attempt to modify 28 points within the law. The veto eliminated, for example, language referring to respect for indigenous groups, compliance by television stations of labor laws and intellectual property rights, and the respect by television stations of pluralism, arguing that other laws already covered these issues. For those involved in the citizens' media movement this represented a blatant disrespect for the work they had done over five years to ensure that this language would be included. Sáez Baeza (2014b) notes that the veto also eliminated the statement that the use of the electromagnetic spectrum should be oriented toward the satisfaction of the collective needs of the public, and that concessionary use of the spectrum would be temporary. Critics argued that the outgoing president was attempting to limit even more severely the rights of the civil sector and to further commercialize Chilean television.[15] From January to March 2014, the law returned to the Senate and the Chamber of Deputies for further consideration, reemerging after another round of voting with less discussion of pluralism, among other points. On May 22, 2014, after six years of debate, and with President Michelle Bachelet back in office, the law was finally promulgated.

## CONCLUSION

A week after the Chamber of Deputies approved the digital television law, I asked Cristián Valdivia, one of Señal 3-La Victoria's founding members, for his opinion on the legislation. He shrugged his shoulders, suggesting that the law no longer concerned him. "We'll keep transmitting," he replied. "It will just be even more underground." When I asked him to explain, he added, "Well, we'll do internet streaming, and we'll keep transmitting via analog." Responding to my puzzled expression, he continued, "I assume a lot of people in the neighborhood won't have digital television for a while, so they'll see it. And even when they do get a digital television, the television in the kitchen or in their bedroom will still be analog." Cristián's words signaled that despite all of the time they had spent educating themselves, politicians, and the public about the digital transition, community television participants and their families would, for the most part,

---

[13] See Sáez Baeza (2013a).
[14] See Observatorio de Medios Fucatel (2013).
[15] See Obervatorio de Medios Fucatel (2014a, 2014b) and Sáez Baeza (2014a, 2014b).

be left waiting for the political and technological changes around which they had been organizing for six years.

In this article, I have argued that community television activists, such as Polo and Cristián, viewed the digital transition as a moment to redefine ideas of democratic access and considered the electromagnetic spectrum to be part of a democratic commons, which, as citizens, they had a right to use. Rather than a conferral of citizenship, however, the digital television transition became yet another situation in which they have found themselves waiting for state representatives to act. In this way, the digital television legislation mirrored the everyday experience of low-income sectors with the state. As Javier Auyero writes in his ethnography focused on the politics of waiting in Argentina, "The state tells its subjects, either implicitly or explicitly, with words or with actions: 'Wait, be patient, and you might benefit from my (reluctant) benevolence'" (2012, p. 14).[16] Whereas their relation to "piracy culture" had enabled community television participants to resolve their day-to-day material and informational needs in a timely way, the path to "legitimate" transmission was one of continual postponement.

In his work on the relation between time and power, Bourdieu writes, "A person can be durably 'held' (so that he can be made to wait, hope, etc.) only to the extent that he is invested in the game so that the complicity of his dispositions can in a sense be counted on" (2000, p. 231). Cristián's response suggested that he was no longer invested in the legislative process. The lack of provision in the law for the infrastructure required for stations like Señal 3 to migrate to the digital system, as well as the lack of guarantee of their access to the spectrum, meant that they had, at least in Cristián's mind, no option other than becoming even more "pirate" than they had been before the digital transition. Piracy, here again, becomes an expression of political subjectivity, indicating Chilean community television's fraught relation with the state over the use and distribution of public goods. Organization around digital television legislation had provided a brief moment in which activists such as those at Señal 3 imagined the possibility of social change in dialogue with the state. However, for these activists, the failure of politicians to recognize the legislation as an opportunity to reaffirm the spaces of political participation that they had fought to obtain became further evidence of the incompleteness of the democratization process. Chile's digital television legislation, according to the citizens' media movement, had not allowed for more innovative ideas regarding media democratization to take hold, but rather had continued the same analog politics. Just as had occurred during the analog era, the community television stations worried that economic, technical, or legal barriers would eventually impede their transmission. Although they had finally achieved recognition from state institutions such as the National Council on Television (CNTV), they still found themselves relying on pirate infrastructure for their projects of social change.

## ACKNOWLEDGMENTS

I am grateful to members of Señal 3 and Canal Pichilemu (especially Polo Lillo, Cristián Valdivia, and Paula Gálvez) for generously allowing me to participate in their activities over the last several years. Harris Solomon, Kathleen Millar, Matthew Gutmann, Catherine Lutz, Kay Warren, and

---

[16]For alternative discussions of how micro-level exchanges express macro-structures of power and inequality, see, for example, Cook and Rice (2006) and Yamagishi, Gillmore, and Cook (1988).

Faye Ginsburg all provided insightful feedback at various stages of the research and writing process. I would also like to thank Patrick Burkart, Jonas Andersson Schwarz, and two anonymous readers for their helpful comments.


## FUNDING

Research for this article was funded by a Fulbright-Hays Doctoral Dissertation Research Abroad Grant, a National Science Foundation Dissertation Improvement Grant, and the Craig M. Cogut Dissertation Fellowship in Latin American & Caribbean Studies.


## REFERENCES

Andersson Schwarz, J. (2012). The quiet agglomeration of data: How piracy is made mundane. *International Journal of Communication, 6*, 585–605. Retrieved from http://ijoc.org/index.php/ijoc/article/view/1213

Auyero, J. (2012). *Patients of the state: The politics of waiting in Argentina*. Durham, NC: Duke University Press.

Balázs, B. (2011). Coda: A short history of book piracy. In J. Karaganis (Ed.), *Media piracy in emerging economies* (pp. 399–413). New York, NY: Social Science Research Council.

Bourdieu, P. (2000). *Pascalian meditations*. Stanford, CA: Stanford University Press.

Bresnahan, R. (2003). The media and the democratic transition in Chile: Democratic promise unfulfilled. *Latin American Perspectives, 30*(6), 39–68. doi:10.1177/0095399703256257

Castells, M., & Cardoso, G. (2012). Piracy cultures: Editorial introduction. *International Journal of Communication, 6*, 826–833. Retrieved from http://ijoc.org/index.php/ijoc/article/viewFile/1610/732

Cook, K., & Rice, E. (2006). Social exchange theory. In J. DeLamater (Ed.), *Handbook of social psychology* (pp. 53–76). New York, NY: Springer.

Dawdy, S. L. (2011). Why pirates are back. *Annual Review of Law and Social Sciences, 7*, 361–385. doi:10.1146/annurev-lawsocsci-102510-105433

Dawdy, S. L., & Bonni, J. (2012). Towards a general theory of piracy. Special collection: Pirates and piracy, broadly conceived. *Anthropological Quarterly, 85*(3), 673–700.

Debate TV Pública en la Era Digital. (2012). *YouTube*. Retrieved from https://www.youtube.com/watch?v=GeLo3qzcyr0

Dent, A. (2012a). Introduction: Understanding the war on piracy, or why we need more anthropology of pirates. Special collection: Pirates and piracy, broadly conceived. *Anthropological Quarterly, 85*(3), 659–672. doi: 10.1353/anq.2012.0040

Dent, A. (2012b). Piracy, circulatory legitimacy, and neoliberal subjectivity in Brazil. *Cultural Anthropology, 27*(1), 28–49. doi:10.1111/j.1548-1360.2011.01125.x

Galperin, H. (2006). Digital broadcasting in the developing world: A Latin American perspective. In M. Cave & K. Nakamura (Eds.), *Digital broadcasting: Policy and practice in the Americas, Europe and Japan* (pp. 39–53). Northampton, MA: Edward Elgar Publishing.

Ginsburg, F., Abu-Lughod, L., & Larkin, B. (2002). Introduction. In F. Ginsburg, L. Abu-Lughod, & B. Larkin (Eds.), *Media worlds: Anthropology on new terrain* (pp. 1–36). Berkeley, CA: University of California Press.

Gobierno de Chile [Government of Chile]. (2013). *Televisión digital abierta y gratuita para Chile* [Free and open access digital television for Chile]. Retrieved from http://www.gob.cl/especiales/television-digital-abierta-y-gratuita-para-chile/

Hardt, M., & Negri, A. (2009). *Commonwealth*. Cambridge, MA: Harvard University Press.

Heller-Roazen, D. (2009). *The enemy of all: Piracy and the law of nations*. New York, NY: Zone Books.

Hess, C., & Ostrom, E. (2006). *Understanding knowledge as a commons: From theory to practice*. Cambridge, MA: MIT Press.

Johns, A. (2009). *Piracy: The intellectual property wars from Gutenberg to Gates*. Chicago, IL: University of Chicago Press.

Karaganis, J. (Ed.). (2011). *Media piracy in emerging economies*. New York, NY: Social Science Research Council.

Lessig, L. (2001). *The future of ideas: The fate of the commons in a connected world*. New York, NY: Random House.

Lessig, L. (2004). *Free culture: How big media uses technology and the law to lock down culture and control creativity*. New York, NY: Penguin Press.

Mesa de la Ciudadanía y TV Digital. (2010). *Proposal of the Mesa de la Ciudadanía y Televisión Digital for more and better television for Chile*. Retrieved from http://www.observatoriofucatel.cl/wp-content/uploads/2010/08/Declaracion_ciudadania-1.pdf

Mesa de Ciudadanía y TV Digital. (n.d.a). *¿Qué proponemos?* Retrieved from http://www.ciudadaniatv.cl/que-proponemos/

Mesa de Ciudadanía y TV Digital. (n.d.b). *Somos*. Retrieved from http://www.ciudadaniatv.cl/somos/

Mylonas, Y. (2012). Piracy culture in Greece: Local realities and civic potentials. *International Journal of Communications, 6*, 710–734. Retrieved from http://ijoc.org/index.php/ijoc/article/view/1190

Observatorio de Medios Fucatel [Media Observatory Fucatel]. (2013, December 20). *Herman Chadwick aborda con Bachelet posibilidad de nueva ley sobre television digital* [Herman Chadwick addresses with Bachelet the possibility of a new law regarding digital television]. [Weblog post]. Retrieved from http://www.observatoriofucatel.cl/herman-chadwick-aborda-con-bachelet-posibilidad-de-nueva-ley-sobre-television-digital/

Observatorio de Medios Fucatel [Media Observatory Fucatel]. (2014a, January 8). *Comisiones Unidas Declararon Inadmisible El Veto a la TV Digital* [Joint Commissions Declared Impermissible Digital TV veto]. Retrieved from http://www.observatoriofucatel.cl/comisiones-unidas-declararon-inadmisible-el-veto-a-la-tv-digital/

Observatorio de Medios Fucatel [Media Observatory Fucatel]. (2014b, January 14). *ChileActores presenta reparos por veto a proyecto de TV digital* [ChileActores present objections to the veto to the Digital TV bill]. Retrieved from http://www.observatoriofucatel.cl/chileactores-presenta-reparos-por-veto-a-proyecto-de-tv-digital/

Poster, M. (2007). Internet piracy as radical democracy? In L. Dahlberg & E. Siapera (Eds.), *Radical democracy and the internet: Interrogating theory and practice* (pp. 207–225). New York, NY: Palgrave Macmillan.

Red de Prensa Popular. (1986). *El Pirata Honrada: Fondo común de dibujos e ilustraciones*. Santiago, Chile: Eco Educación y Comunicaciones.

Red de Televisiones Populares de Chile demanda a la Presidenta. (2009, May 5). *El Ciudadano*. Retrieved from http://www.elciudadano.cl/2009/05/05/7712/red-de-televisiones-populares-de-chile-demanda-a-la-presidenta/

Rozas, D. (2008, December 8). *¿Fin de transmisiones?: Señal 3 La Victoria corre peligro de desaparecer* [End of Transmissions?: Señal 3 La Victoria runs the risk of disappearing]. Retrieved from http://www.rebelion.org/noticia.php?id=77153

Sáez Baeza, C. (2014a, April). *Chile: la TV Digital en el Purgatorio* [Chile: TV Digital in Purgatory]. [Weblog]. Retrieved from http://observacom.org/chile-la-tv-digital-en-el-purgatorio/

Sáez Baeza, C. (2014b, January 6). *Controversia por veto presidencial contra ley digital* [Controversy over presidential veto of digital TV law]. [Weblog]. Retrieved from http://www.uchile.cl/noticias/97968/chiara-saez-controversia-por-veto-presidencial-contra-ley-tvdigital

Sáez Baeza, C. (2013a, October 22). *Ley de TV Digital: lo que el gobierno omite* [Digital TV Law: What the government omits]. [Weblog post]. Retrieved from http://www.sentidoscomunes.cl/ley-de-tv-digital-lo-que-el-gobierno-omite/

Sáez Baeza, C. (2013b). Políticas públicas de comunicación y participación ciudadana: el caso de la television digital en Chile [Public policies regarding communication and citizen participation: The case of digital television in Chile]. *Signo y Pensamiento 63 – Agendas XXXII*, 34–51. Retrieved from http://revistas.javeriana.edu.co/index.php/signoypensamiento/article/viewFile/6941/5518

Skinner, R. (2012). Artists, music piracy, and the crisis of political subjectivity in contemporary Mali. *Anthropological Quarterly, 85*(3), 723–754. doi:10.1353/anq.2012.0053

Spilker, H. S. (2012). The network studio revisited: Becoming an artist in the age of "piracy cultures." *International Journal of Communication, 6*, 773–794. Retrieved from http://ijoc.org/index.php/ijoc/article/view/1087/730

Tironi, E., & Sunkel, G. (2001). *Concentración económica de los medios* [Economic concentration of the media]. Santiago, Chile: LOM Ediciones.

Yamagishi, T., Gillmore, M., & Cook, K. (1988). Network connections and the distribution of power in exchange networks. *American Journal of Sociology, 93*(4), 833–851.

# Piracy, Geoblocking, and Australian Access to Niche Independent Cinema

Rebecca Beirne

*University of Newcastle*

Online audiovisual piracy cannot be properly understood if divorced from its context. This article uses the availability of lesbian-focused films in Australia as a lens through which to consider the relationship between online audiovisual piracy and industry geoblocking practices. It is argued that artificial control through internet geoblocking can limit potential global sales by restricting universal availability of certain films. Anti-piracy discourses around lost sales and reduced profits for film industries are complicated by piracy contexts where there is no mechanism for viewers to make legal online purchases. When looking beyond Hollywood, the diverse purposes of independent and minority filmmakers provide a more complex understanding of piracy overall. This article proposes a more nuanced approach to online film piracy that emphasizes context, taking into consideration that pirate culture is formed by an extensive but inchoate network of individuals with diffuse motivations that have differential impacts upon the industry.

Audiovisual piracy is more complex and contextual than anti-piracy discourses, promulgated by industries and governments, would have us believe. Although audiovisual piracy does have negative impacts, there are pirate practices that many would view in a radically different way than mainstream framings of piracy as theft or at least causing harm to the industry. In some cases, internet film piracy can perform an important role in opening up access to film texts constricted by globally unequal constraints on consumers. The recent documentary *North Korea: Life Inside the Secret State* (Jones, 2013), for example, depicts individuals risking their lives to distribute and acquire Hollywood films and television shows on DVD. With no legal means of purchasing international media and entertainment, these individuals are not depriving studios of their funds, and their activities seem more likely to be frameworked as political than criminal. This is not a unique situation. In 1980s' Romania, for example, "films accessed through pirated VHS tapes definitely helped shape the Romanian people's resistance to the political status quo by offering at least a glimpse of a desirable alternative" (Dwyer & Uricaru, 2009, p. 48). Such contexts are not disappearing in the present day. Russia's 2013 law changes prohibiting the distribution of material that "may cause a 'distorted understanding' that gay and heterosexual relations are 'socially equivalent'" to heterosexual relationships ("Russia's Vladimir Putin," 2013) are likely to cause significant illegal trading of gay and lesbian film texts. Are the ethics, or at least, the

33

*harm* of audiovisual piracy subject to context? While film industries worldwide have broadened their "piracy = theft" messages to a variety of campaigns (see Parkes, 2013), in Australia legislative and industry messages continue to emphasize that illegal physical and internet-based piracy financially damages the film industry to the point of costing local jobs.

This article uses the online distribution in Australia of films with lesbian lead characters—both a genre and niche independent industry, chosen for its appeal to a small but globally diverse audience—as a case study to examine the role played by geoblocking in restricting access to small independent films. I argue that geoblocking practices encourage online film piracy, making piracy a central (sometimes the only) means of enabling wider distribution of important cultural texts to a minority audience for whom it may be difficult or impossible to purchase some films legally. Globally dissimilar access to film texts is not a new situation, and has been examined through the discourse of "piracy as access" by postcolonial scholars "interested in the transformative aspects of piracy, in piracy's capacity to disseminate culture, knowledge and capital" (Lobato, 2012, p. 82). Building on discussions that primarily centre on pirate DVD networks, I see online geoblocking as an extension and intensification of practices that create international differences in access to film texts where there is no geographical rationale to do so. The small yet global industry of lesbian-focused filmmaking and distribution has a dispersed international potential audience base for whom questions of access are also political. Through engaging with this industry, I contend that online piracy that emerges from a context of geoblocking, where denial of access has been enforced at an industrial level, is a unique form of piracy, one that I will henceforth refer to as geo-access piracy. There are multiple convincing articulations of piracy, synthesized recently by Brown (2014). Therefore, it is a mistake for film industries to approach diverse forms of piracy in exactly the same way, identifying consumers as the only issue. In some cases, such as that of geo-access piracy, it is the industry itself that has established arbitrary barriers to the purchase of its products.

A relatively new dimension of the film industry, independent films featuring lesbian characters with an implied lesbian audience began circulating on the gay and lesbian film festival circuit in the early-mid 1990s (see Beirne, 2014, p. 130). With a few notable exceptions, such as studio-independents *Bound, Imagine Me and You,* and *The Kids Are Alright,* lesbian-focused films exist outside mainstream film distribution flows, relying on a small number of distributors marketing these films to a same-sex desiring female audience. The majority of these distributors are situated in specific geographic locations, particularly the United States and some European nations (Beirne, 2014, p. 131). While the industry that distributes lesbian-focused films is small and concentrated, a niche minority audience for these films is scattered around the globe. In 1978, Richard Dyer emphasized the importance for lesbian and gay audiences of viewing gay characters on film who were "ordinary" and free from stereotype (paras. 10, 23), and these ideas have infused popular and academic critique of lesbian and gay images on screen ever since. For most of film history, lesbian and female bisexual characters have either been absent from the silver screen or represented in negative ways (see Cairns, 2006; Weiss, 1992; Whatling, 1997; White, 1999; Wilton, 1995). While a handful of television series feature same-sex-desiring female protagonists and mainstream film texts are more likely to present same-sex desire in minor female characters in a more positive way, they still only rarely include lesbian or bisexual women and their relationships as the main characters or narratives. To view films with narratives focused on same-sex desiring female protagonists (hereafter called lesbian-focused films), viewers must generally turn to the growing number of independent small and micro-budget productions that are being made all around the world. As a marginal part of the film industry that primarily distributes online (via DVD delivery or digitally) and almost never achieves widescale theatrical exhibition, lesbian-focused film would seem particularly vulnerable to any reductions in sales caused by digital piracy. Where the anti-piracy discourse that characterizes such filmmakers as "struggling artists" focuses on the profit-making dimension of online piracy (see Swan, 2007; Seidler, 2010), there is little consideration of why these films are being pirated or how wider, conglomerate-industry practices, enforced globally by the US government through trade deals (Dorling, 2013), contribute to a situation that weakens the ability of independent distributors to compete with copyright infringing distribution and even encourages piracy of their films.

Unfortunately for a small industry targeting a global consumer base, geo-blocking means that there are lesbian-focused films that cannot be readily purchased for download or streaming in some nations. While many such titles can be purchased and shipped on DVD from North America or Western Europe, this is a slow and costly enterprise that is not a true competitor to the imme-diacy of streaming or downloading, nor a deterrent to pirating. For viewers exclusively engaged with the online market, there is no alternative to piracy if one wishes to access a number of these films online in countries such as Australia. The situation becomes even more difficult in nations with a harsher approach to lesbian relationships, rights and identities where it may also be problematic to order DVDs. Moving from a consumer to an industry perspective, the inability of potential consumers to purchase goods-for-sale has significant implications in terms of lost revenue, something these often small-scale productions cannot afford. In the context of lesbian-focused cinema, which has a role to play for a marginalized minority beyond simple commercial entertainment, lack of access to these films also compounds invisibility. The enormous illegal grey-economy of online pirate film distribution makes a number of films available to consumers who would otherwise never have an opportunity to watch them. While uploaders to bittorrent, newsgroup, or online streaming sites make these films accessible to both audiences who do and do not have access to paid services, downloaders and streamers from nonpurchasable contexts are not depriving the distributors of product or potential income, so it is neither accurate nor legiti-mate to characterize them within the discourse of pirate-as-thief. This article contends that pirate distribution of lesbian-focused films has a role to play in making them accessible to interested individuals around the world, and furthermore, that mainstream media discourses about digital piracy are too simplistic, particularly in the context of geoblocking.

## UNDERSTANDING PIRACY

Piracy is a loaded term. Once used to describe groups of armed high-sea bandits robbing iso-lated and vulnerable individuals, it has now become the dominant descriptor for individuals who duplicate, distribute and/or consume copyrighted material. Digital pirates, those who upload, download, or stream audiovisual, music, software, or other files from the internet have been under particular scrutiny over the last decade. Defining piracy is not a straightforward venture, and "given the existence of 'multiple piracies,' the singular term piracy is manifestly inadequate to describe [digital piracy]" (Brown, 2014, p. 132). The meaning includes multiple categories of individuals: those who duplicate legal products (whether for sale or not), those who facili-tate the dissemination of unauthorized copies of files (for business or other reasons), and those who acquire and consume these files and who may or may not then redistribute them (passively or actively). Functioning outside the established, naturalized economic and legal order, the "pirate" is complex, difficult to define, and impossible to pin down. Attempts to control the definition within both legal and public discourse are inherently ideological, with wider community practices not always congruent with the desires of industry. As both interested parties and shapers of public opinion, film and television industries are part of the rhetorical battle to define piracy, and their attempts to counter and control it have been well-documented (see, e.g., Lewis, 2007; Parkes, 2013; Waterman, Ji, & Rochet, 2007). Industry bodies have been known to take such definitional unrest to extremes through aligning audiovisual piracy with more established icons of crime through "claiming connections between movie 'piracy,' 'organized crime,' and even 'terrorist' organizations" (Yar, 2005, p. 678). The alleged harm being done to film industries is another popular element of anti-piracy education campaigns, and the emergence of law firms in the United Kingdom, United States, and Germany specializing in "speculative invoicing mass/volume litigation of peer-to-peer pirates" (Lobato & Thomas, 2012, p. 618) demonstrates a wider acceptance of this definition of pirates as "those who damage film industries," a more subjective characterization than "those who profit from copyright infringement."

Michael Parkes's work on anti-piracy campaigns in the United Kingdom documents a shift away from straightforward piracy as theft discourses. In the case of Australia, the highlighting of piracy as theft and the harm caused by lost sales, remains central to the anti-piracy discourse of dominant industry organizations. In 2007, for example, the chief executive officer (CEO) of the Australian Federation Against Copyright Theft (AFACT) drew direct links between DVD piracy and organized crime while also reinforcing piracy's potential role in the loss of Australian film industry jobs ("Burning issue," 2007). In 2011, the CEO of The Intellectual Property Awareness Foundation (IPAF) reasserted that "it is theft. Let's start defining it as theft" (Swift, 2011). Meanwhile, AFACT and major distributor Village Roadshow pursued internet service provider (ISP) iiNET through the courts in an attempt to force the company to prevent its customers from bittorrenting. Village Roadshow lost both the case and their appeal to the High Court ("Hollywood studios lose," 2012), indicating a lack of congruence between their perspectives and Australian law. However, by 2014 the industry's subsequent lobbying of the Australian government, together with "provisions concerning copyright" in negotiations with "major trading partners" (Brandis, 2014) has resulted in the consideration of a series of legislative measures ranging from forcing ISPs to block or take down copyright infringing websites or through to the introduction of controversial "three strikes" legislation (Hutchinson, 2014).

Perspectives that seek to determine how piracy damages the film industry, or strategize how to eliminate it, are both based on the assumption that online piracy is a threat to the film industry, sometimes even to its very survival. Astronomical loss figures are often cited by industry organizations, and scholars are also not immune from attempting to calculate losses in a market and situation where it is almost impossible to gain representative data. Arther S. De Vany and W. David Walls (2007), for example, have developed a model for estimating the "losses" caused by piracy based on the data about *one* Hollywood film, data furnished by an invested industry. Some scholars, however, question the extent to which the industry is truly suffering. Majid Yar, for example, rightly warns that "statistics supporting a supposed near-exponential increase in 'piracy' need to be treated with considerable caution" (2005, p. 678) while some "show that there are conditions under which piracy could make the profit of the firm increase" (Dejean, 2009, p. 327). There is also ongoing growth in box office income (Hughes, 2014; MPAA, 2013).

It must be also be remembered that box office figures, oft quoted as a measure of a film's success or failure, are only one part of the story and DVD, Blu-Ray, television, download, merchandise, and other sales need to be considered. In 2013, for example, films bought for at-home viewing equaled $18.2 billion while "digital purchases of movies are increasing so rapidly they will have eclipsed slumping DVD sales by the end of 2014" (Garrahan, 2014). Piracy has primarily been discussed in relation to Hollywood, though a few scholars have considered it in relation to independent or niche film (e.g., Moore, 2013). It is important to note that the models used to examine piracy in relation to Hollywood cinema are not universally applicable. This is due to a variety of differences. First, the common practice of evaluating piracy in terms of box office losses does not make sense for films that do not have widespread (or even any) theatrical release, and make most of their income from DVD or online sales—platforms not protected by the cinema experience (Dejean, 2009, p. 342). By primarily examining mainstream/Hollywood films, one can fall into discussing piracy as if it is a singular force. The way online film piracy is understood by industry bodies is fundamentally flawed because film piracy is contextual, not universal. Piracy takes different forms, there are a diversity of pirates, they have different levels of impact on the film industry, and there are reasons why a viewership imperative may outweigh a profit motive in some contexts.

In August 2012 the founder of SurftheChannel.com, a site providing links to streaming legal and illegal video, was jailed ("Pirate website owner," 2012). This was by no means the first prosecution of a video pirate. However, the case was remarkable as Anton Vickerman's incarceration was the result of a private prosecution by the UK iteration of industry group FACT, and based on "conspiracy to defraud" laws. As such, it was part of "ongoing attempts to move copyright violation from the realm of 'regulatory offences' and into the domain of (morally stigmatized) *criminal* conduct" (Yar, 2005, p. 684, emphasis in original). While multiple industry and government advertising campaigns portray pirates as either thieves or dealers in stolen merchandise, digital piracy is widespread among ordinary citizens, for whom "copyright violations have been rendered socially acceptable by their ubiquity and the widespread perception that they are not genuinely 'harmful' in the manner of 'real crimes'"(Yar, 2005, p. 687). The question of how much is being "lost," however, remains a common preoccupation. In Vickerman's trial, industry representatives were not suing for the loss of goods, but rather the amorphous loss of *potential* sales. Vickerman's conviction of conspiracy to defraud, for example, was based on a loss figure furnished by FACT of "between £52m and £198m, on the basis that 55% of those who watched films via the site might instead have seen it in the cinema, rented a DVD or otherwise paid for it" (Halliday, 2012). Like the judge in this case, I would classify such figures as "somewhat speculative" (Halliday, 2012). Aside from anything else, it fails to acknowledge that consumers had the option of viewing most of the files elsewhere on the internet if they did not have access to them via SurftheChannel, and that the removal of a links site does not automatically remove the videos themselves from the web.

Framing digital piracy in terms of lost sales also opens up a loophole that the industry has yet to address adequately. If someone could download or stream a file *without* impacting potential sales, how can it be considered as equivalent to other forms of piracy? In the context of global geoblocking, if distributors are not providing consumers with a way to buy the product, and pirating it thus cannot possibly result in a loss of sales, and certainly does not result in the loss of a product (as with all duplication-based piracy), can we really still consider it theft? Contemporary discourses of film as merely product, clearly reinforced by industry and governments, fail to address the sociopolitical importance of some forms of film beyond commercial consideration, in this case, lesbian-themed film. Within the context of geoblocking, distributors closing down pirate websites and channels making these films freely available effectively make socially transgressive films of significant importance for a minority community inaccessible to certain international audiences who were never potential consumers in the first place. This is also the case for young people without access to credit cards and far away from large or specialty physical retail shops that might stock these titles, many of which are films close to impossible to find even in major cosmopolitan cities. Although a threat to the industry that funds and produces lesbian-focused films, piracy provides one (sometimes the only) space for the open dissemination of these films to a geographically dispersed audience. In so doing, internet piracy plays a role as an agent of popular cultural social change by flattening the audience class system created by geoblocking. It is a system that disproportionately disadvantages nonmainstream films, which are much less likely to garner sufficient, or large enough scale, distribution to achieve worldwide release.

Limited release patterns are common for lesbian-focused films due to their independent funding structure and reliance on smaller niche distributors who generally only have national or regional rights. A film must usually secure a separate distributor for each sales territory, and anything outside these areas will generally go unexploited. Outside the dominant territories of the United States and Western Europe, distributor numbers, and number of films released, are finite. With one or two exceptions, even cult favorites are not easily available worldwide. While many titles can be ordered from the United States or Europe on DVD, delivery timeframes and the high cost of shipping render this kind of product a weak competitor for illegal download or instant streaming for audiences with on-demand expectations. Large paid download providers such as iTunes also have few titles available, as they will not accept small distributors as suppliers. As of the time of writing, Netflix, which hosts a number of lesbian-focused films, was available to potential subscribers in most of North and South America and is gradually expanding into Western Europe. However, the majority of European nations, and all of Asia, Africa, and Australasia, are still not able to purchase the service. User complaints also indicate that, much like iTunes, the selection of titles in the stores outside the United States is significantly reduced—even Canadian viewers have 6,000 fewer titles to choose from than their neighbors (Fitzgerald, 2014). Other large global concerns such as Amazon Instant Video (which stocks a number of titles in this genre) are geoblocked to those outside the United States, United Kingdom, Germany, and Japan. Access to films on smaller distributor-owned (WolfeOnDemand) or third-party sites (BlinkBox, Busk) that host lesbian-focused films is also generally only available in particular countries. This places limitations on online download and streaming sales and rentals, and thus on the production and marketing budgets of subsequent films. Films, even of the low budget, independent variety, cost a lot of money to make, market, and distribute, with many non-Hollywood filmmakers from around the world relying on government grants (*Spider Lilies, This Kiss*), crowdsourcing (*Hannah Free, Submerge*), and even personal funds (*Do I Love You?*) to create their work. Concerns about activities such as piracy that may leach funds from these financially and culturally marginal productions are perfectly legitimate. The filmmakers, however, often have broader political and social concerns that go beyond the simply commercial, which makes providing access to these film texts an important element in addition to profit.

Looking at a sample of films that represent the niche subgenre of independent lesbian-focused feature films, some producers and directors have espoused ideals beyond making profit, and their funding models would seem to back these up. *Hannah Free* (2009), for example, relied on personal fundraising from members of Chicago's lesbian, gay, bisexual, and transgender communities (T. Baim, personal interview, 2008). *Submerge* (2013), not only offered members of the public walk on roles or private screenings in exchange for donations via their website, but used crowdfunding portal Pozible to raise completion funds. PowerUp, the production company behind *Itty Bitty Titty Committee* (2007) is run as a nonprofit. Ligy J. Pullappally not only self-funded the $1 million feature *The Journey* but also negotiated with her distributors to personally retain rights to the film in India so that it could be screened for free by community or political groups (personal interview, 2008). Taiwanese director Zero Chou has stated that although it was not financially beneficial, she was pleased that illegal copying in China was leading to more individuals seeing *Spider Lilies* (2007; Lo, 2008, para. 10). Despite being an arthouse film with a narrative focused on lesbian characters, *Spider Lilies* ranked fifth in underground film sales in China in 2007, reaching viewers who would otherwise never have had access to it had they relied on the official film economy. None of these filmmakers would have anticipated a significant financial return on their work, with some unlikely to even recoup costs. There was a value placed by multiple individuals on having these films in the world, a value that was not solely monetary. These kinds of attitudes to funding and distribution reveal a different, minority independent perspective on the purposes of filmmaking to that promulgated by major studios whose investments are more purely commercial than political and emotional. The impact of piracy should also be measured against these other kinds of factors. In Chou's case, her desire for mainland Chinese audiences to see her film have at least ameliorated the profit motive. I contend that such contexts need to be taken into consideration, and geo-access piracy cannot be adequately addressed by industry approaches to piracy that solely focus on the consumer.

## AUSTRALIA AND ACCESS

For a wealthy nation with a small population, Australia boasts a disproportionately large number of illegal downloaders (see "Australians named worst," 2012; "Breaking bad," 2013). Several interrelated factors contribute to this situation. First, Australian residents pay significantly more for the same digitally downloaded or streamed products than their counterparts around the globe (Yeates, 2012). Elevated costs paid for physical products can be explained somewhat by the high cost of shipping to Australia, but consumers are resentful about paying DVD prices or even more for a product that does not have to be transported anywhere and costs no more to supply or market.[1] The additional delay in release times for films and television episodes certainly do not improve matters. A further issue for viewers seeking films beyond standard Hollywood fare is the extremely limited distribution of independent and niche film products. When national consumer groups such as Choice publish guides on how to "beat" geoblocking via Virtual Private Networks and Domain Name System re-routers ("Circumventing geo-blocking," 2013), it clearly signifies either a resistance to purchase from existing online digital video retailers, whether international (iTunes, Google Play) or local (BigPond Movies, Quickflix), or a acknowledgement that the desired titles are simply not available through these services. While Australians have been

---

[1] In early May 2014, for example, mass discount retail chain JB Hi-Fi was selling Disney's *Frozen* on DVD for AUD$15.98 (with 99 cent shipping to metropolitan locations). iTunes Australia was selling *Frozen* downloads for the higher price of $19.99, though Google Play priced the film at $14.99.

subject to the same kinds of advertising campaigns as US consumers (including the famous "You wouldn't steal a car" prefeature warning on DVDs) and discourses surrounding film downloading construct it within a discourse of theft and harm, there exists a counter-awareness that the population is being exploited by studios and online distributors, and is denied access to products readily purchasable elsewhere in the world. The result is a sanctioning of illegal downloading as a reasonable and socially acceptable practice. As Stuart P. Green has observed "criminal law is least effective—and least legitimate—when it is at odds with widely held moral intuitions" (2012, p. 2), and the morality of complying with those who put national locks on a global platform, and endorsing an unequivalent system through voluntary participation, is counterintuitive indeed.

Despite Choice's suggestion, knowledge of anti-geoblocking services is still not widespread, and a degree of technological know-how is generally required, making them inaccessible to many casual consumers. In early December 2013 I attempted to determine whether there are particular lesbian-focused films that are challenging to acquire via paid services in Australia. My choice of films for this case study were those that potential consumers might find out about through aggregate lists on popular websites and then search for online. The first selections were from a 2012 user-voted top 20 list on Afterellen.com—the biggest website focused on popular culture featuring lesbians and bisexual women (owned by MTV Networks/Viacom). Additional films from the largest independent lesbian-entertainment site, Autostraddle, were then added. To supplement these sources, Google searches were conducted for "top lesbian films" and "best lesbian independent films," with the 20 titles suggested by Google as "movies frequently mentioned on the web" added to the selection of titles (December 6, 2013). Having established a final list of 39 feature films, I attempted to locate these films on the main Australian-accessible paid websites for film streaming and download purchase (see Table 1). Further sites directed at Australian audiences were surveyed, but these were either obscure and included either no or only a limited number of relevant titles (e.g., Mubi which offers a rotation of independent cinema, with only 30 titles offered at any given time), or required investment in additional hardware, such as Foxtel or Fetch TV (essentially Pay Television providers with an on-demand online service). Five sites were selected for survey: iTunes Australia and BigPond Movies as the most prominent players in the industry, Quickflix as the largest Australian-owned streaming service, and Google Play as a newer but very visible player. An additional US-distributor site, Wolfe on Demand, was added. Although the majority of their lesbian-focused films have not always been accessible from Australia (see Beirne, 2014, p. 135), this appears to have been recently rectified.

As can be seen in Table 1, 17 of the 39 films were available for rental and/or purchase on the various websites (iTunes 9, Google Play 5, BigPond 4, Wolfe on Demand 3, and Quickflix 1). Twenty-two films were not available on any of these sites, about 56% of the sample. While previous examinations of UK and US paid sites revealed limitations on what could be accessed (Beirne, 2014), the variety of titles offered in that study far exceeded the Australian sample. With enough searching it is possible to find some of these films on imported DVD in Australia (most Australian-made films in this genre are also distributed by overseas companies), or more commonly, to have them shipped from overseas at significant expense. A handful of retail stores in metropolitan areas do stock lesbian-focused DVDs, several of which also offer online DVD sales. The Bookshop Darlinghurst in central Sydney, for example, stocks 8 of the 39 titles available with prices ranging from $12.99 to $39.99 plus shipping from $8.25 (depending on speed of delivery). Australian online retailer Fishpond has a larger number of (often cheaper) lesbian-focused films

TABLE 1
Australian Online Availability and Cost of Popular Films With Lesbian Lead Characters

| | iTunes Australia | BigPond | Quickflix | Google Play | Wolfe on Demand |
|---|---|---|---|---|---|
| Aimee and Jaguar | no | no | no | no | no |
| All Over Me | no | no | no | no | no |
| Better than Chocolate | no | no | no | no | no |
| Bound | no | no | no | no | no |
| Boys Don't Cry | $4.99R/$17.99B | $3.99R | no | no | no |
| But I'm a Cheerleader | no | $3.99R | no | no | no |
| Chasing Amy | $4.99R/$14.99B | no | no | $3.99R/$9.99B | no |
| Chutney Popcorn | no | no | no | no | no |
| D.E.B.S. | $4.99R/$14.99B | $3.99R | no | $3.99R/$12.99B | no |
| Desert Hearts | no | no | no | no | no |
| Elena Undone | no | no | no | no | US$3.99R/$14.99B |
| Fingersmith | no | no | no | no | no |
| Fire | no | no | no | no | no |
| Gia | no | no | no | no | no |
| Go Fish | no | no | no | no | no |
| Heavenly Creatures | $4.99R/$14.99B | no | no | $3.99R/$9.99B | no |
| High Art | no | no | subscription | no | no |
| I Can't Think Straight | $6.99R/$24.99B | no | no | no | no |
| If These Walls Could Talk 2 | no | no | no | no | no |
| Imagine Me and You | no | no | no | no | no |
| It's in the Water | no | no | no | no | US$3.99R/$14.99B |
| Itty Bitty Titty Committee | no | no | no | no | no |
| Jamie and Jessie Are Not Together | no | no | no | no | no |
| Kiss Me | no | no | no | no | no |
| Kissing Jessica Stein | $4.99R/$17.99B | $3.99R | no | no | no |
| Lianna | no | no | no | no | no |
| Lost and Delirious | no | no | no | no | no |
| Loving Annabelle | no | no | no | no | no |
| Mulholland Drive | no | no | no | no | no |
| My Summer of Love | $4.99R/$11.99B | no | no | $3.99R/$14.99B | no |
| Puccini for Beginners | no | no | no | no | no |
| Saving Face | $4.99R/$14.99B | no | no | $3.99R/$12.99B | no |
| Show Me Love | no | no | no | no | no |
| The Incredibly True Adventures | no | no | no | no | no |
| The Watermelon Woman | no | no | no | no | no |
| The World Unseen | $6.99R/$24.99B | no | no | no | no |
| Tipping the Velvet | no | no | no | no | no |
| Water Lilies | no | no | no | no | no |
| When Night is Falling | no | no | no | no | US$3.99R/$14.99B |

on DVD, and offers free shipping. Unfortunately, availability is premised on outsourced distribution. Without local distributors for many of these titles, most of the products on offer are region 1 or 2 DVDs that ship from the United States or United Kingdom, so while the shipping is free, delivery times range from two weeks to over a month. To invest this kind of time and/or money in a film one may or may not enjoy requires a strong commitment to acquiring films. Some consumers, of course, do so, but only legal online purchases can really compete with the immediacy and convenience of online piracy, as the music industry has recognized in recent years. For viewers trying to find lesbian-focused films online in Australia, having viewed all there is to offer on iTunes or BigPond, or even the 17 combined films across all sites, piracy would seem a logical alternative to source these films.

This is especially the case for those films falling outside the paradigm of studio independents. As would be expected, most of the films available on the major Australian paid sites have studio distribution (*Heavenly Creatures, Boys Don't Cry, Chasing Amy, D.E.B.S., High Art*), or are released by major independents such as Lionsgate (*But I'm a Cheerleader*; now distributor of films such as *The Hunger Games* series). It is notable that the studio films feature narratives, such as female same-sex desire in the context of obsession and murder (*Heavenly Creatures*), a bisexual woman through the perspective of a male character (*Chasing Amy*), and a relationship between a transsexual man and heterosexual woman (*Boys Don't Cry*). The only smaller scale productions available for purchase or rental are *The World Unseen* and *I Can't Think Straight*. A number of widely distributed and quite mainstream cult-classic studio independents were not available, including the Wachowski's mob thriller *Bound* (1996) or British romantic comedy *Imagine Me and You* (2005). The three films hosted by Wolfe on Demand (*When Night is Falling, Elena Undone, It's in the Water*), while lower budget, still represent fairly standard Hollywood genres (two romances and a quirky romantic comedy). Considering that these films are all drawn from the most popular catalogs, this is to be expected, although there are films within the genre of lesbian-focused cinema that still embrace lo-fi aesthetics and challenging narratives, and these are being distributed through other means, including (legally and illegally) online.

With uncertain and sometimes nonexistent financial returns, truly independent niche films have little buffer room for lost potential sales. Moore contends that "piracy arguably affects whether low-budget filmmakers lucky enough to garner distribution can make enough return on their investment to continue making films" (2013, p. 140). There is also, however, less of a sense that large financial returns are the sole purpose of filmmaking and distribution. Both of these factors need to be taken into consideration when discussing piracy and independent filmmaking. Unfortunately, it is only the former that has been focused on by a mainstream industry keen to shout "will somebody please think of the independents?" in the ideological war on piracy. Writing on the Directors Guild of America website, Andrew Keen laments that "*The Kids Are All Right* ($4 million budget, $34.7 million gross [theatrical]) was downloaded 292,596 times [during February 12–March 7, 2011]. That represents serious revenue loss for [a film] that can ill afford it" (2011). Although representing a niche genre as a lesbian-focused film, *The Kids Are All Right*, made and distributed by one of the largest media companies in the world (Focus Features/Universal Studios), is hardly an independent production. Neither is $30.7 million a tiny outcome, especially as this figure does not take into consideration ongoing income from ancillary sales (e.g., DVDs, pay TV, download). However, it is certainly true that titles made and distributed by smaller companies, without an Oscar buzz or Hollywood marketing campaign, have an uphill battle to attract paying customers, even without facing the competition of bittorrent networks, streaming services, or Usenet.

So how does digital piracy affect the small and micro-budget productions that form a significant part of the genre of lesbian-focused film? This is a difficult question to answer. Independent film producer Barry Sission suggests that "it's hard to say how much file sharing impacts the bottom line. . . . Every production and every marketing campaign is different" (in Sandoval, 2010). An example of a campaign against copyright infringement within the niche industry of lesbian-focused feature film has been *And Then Came Lola* (2009), an independent feature with a budget of just US$250,000. *And Then Came Lola* was fortunate to secure local and European distribution deals with some of the most significant names in queer film distribution: Wolfe Video (United States), Peccadillo Pictures (United Kingdom), Optimale (France), Pro-Fun Media Filmverleih (Germany), and Homescreen (Netherlands). Unfortunately, however, "within 24 hours of its release [in Germany], an unauthorized copy appeared online" (Sandoval, 2010). This led to co-director Seidler taking part in an unusual joint suit with the producers of *The Hurt Locker* and others against internet service providers to obtain the names of individuals who have uploaded or downloaded their films (Mick, 2011). The lawsuit sought compensation from a huge number of individual filesharers/downloaders at a rate of $2,000 per up/download (Mick, 2011). Seidler has since dedicated herself to a battle against piracy, sending Digital Millennium Copyright Act (DMCA) notices and campaigning against Google and other major companies for advertising on websites engaging in copyright infringement. It is interesting that Seidler herself admits on this site that *And Then Came Lola* was "highly successful," undermining the claims made about the damage to the financial viability of this film (Sandoval, 2010). Piracy is not crashing independent filmmakers onto the rocks of extinction, at least not within the genre of lesbian-focused film, as the numbers of filmmakers and volume of films has increased exponentially since the 2000s (see Beirne, 2014, p. 130), at the same time as online audiovisual piracy has truly come of age.

Seidler's argument that "online piracy isn't about altruism, it's about income" (2010) fails to take into account that there *are* those who upload without financial gain. Frequenting forums while researching *The L Word* when it was first screening in 2004, the excitement of viewers to see each new episode of the first lesbian-focused television series was incredible. A good number of these prospective viewers resided in nations outside the United States and were thus unable to purchase a Showtime subscription in order to view and discuss the episodes in line with US viewers. Each week without fail one of the US site members would upload a grainy copy of the episode to file-sharing site YouSendIt and post the link for others to download. Whenever such a copy was removed in the name of copyright, another poster who had already accessed the file would make it available to others. None of these uploaders had any potential to make money out of their "theft" or the redistribution of stolen goods. At most, community goodwill and social capital could be gained as nonmonetary profits that do not easily translate into broader, off-line life. Judging by the accompanying appeals from the file hosts to buy the DVDs when they came out in order to financially support the show, and later posts about boxsets and merchandise, many of these viewers could be identified as "explorers," those consumers whose piracy correlates with a higher number of purchases (Bounie, Bourreau, & Waelbroeck, 2005, pp. 23–24). Although downloaders from torrent sites are being targeted as pirate distributors in speculative invoicing cases, these are often further example of pirates who are not making money out of their uploading, with bartering being a closer analogy. Indeed, with bittorrent file sharing, continuing to upload to others once the file has been successfully obtained, puts the average downloader in further danger of prosecution. There is no profit even in the form of identified social capital (as bittorrent is usually anonymous), and so it does seem an act of reciprocal altruism for the good of the functioning of the bittorrent ecosystem. While not discounting the fact that filmmakers, studios, and television networks do need to generate profits in order to fund subsequent projects, it does seem that pirate uploaders have created a worldwide library of audiovisual content that some viewers would not otherwise be able to see. Some viewers will go on to buy them when and if available, some will not.

Aerlyn Weissman, co-director of feature historical documentary *Forbidden Love*, articulated a passion for the creation and preservation of lesbian-focused cinema:

> When you look at some of the great flowerings of queer culture in the 12th century in Europe, the Weimar Republic; those cultures were effectively destroyed within a very, very short period of time. . . . Our histories are erased, and they've been erased over and over. This was certainly one of my projects in the back of my mind in an era of mass media: they're not going to be able to get every copy of *Forbidden Love*. Our history will live on because there are too many copies of it now, it can't be erased the same way that the newspapers and personal histories, and the chronicles and the journals and what little film there was of the Weimar era is gone; that can't happen again. That gives me enormous satisfaction when I do these films to know they can't erase our culture ever again. It's just not possible. Even if they went after us there's always going to be a DVD in somebody's drawer that tells our stories again. (Personal interview, 2008)

Now circulating the internet both legally in the United States and illegally globally, *Forbidden Love* is not only impossible to destroy but, unlike that DVD copy sitting in a drawer, also impossible to stop people accessing. Unearthing these kinds of attitudes contributes to the richness of the purposes we see for cinema, one that goes beyond the contemporary studio outcry about the death of the film industry at the hands of pirates, and creates a more nuanced understanding of why people make films, as well as how people distribute and watch them. Not every uploader or individual host of a streaming video is motivated by profit, and not every downloaded film loses sales for film industries. Generalizations about piracy do not help industries combat them, and these generalizations certainly do not help us understand the complex phenomenon of geo-access piracy, particularly in relation to independent productions.

## REFERENCES

Australians named worst Game of Thrones pirates. (2012, May 21). *News.com.au*. Retrieved from http://www.news.com.au/technology/australians-named-worst-offenders-for-illegally-download-game-of-thrones/story-e6frfro0-122636215818

Beirne, R. (2014). New queer cinema 2.0? Lesbian-focused films and the internet. *Screen*, *55*(1), 129–138.

Bounie, D., Bourreau, M., & Waelbroeck, P. (2005). *Pirates of explorers? Analysis of music consumption in French graduate schools*. The Second Conference on Information and Knowledge Technology, Tehran, Iran. Retrieved from http://zinc.zew.de/pub/zew-docs/veranstaltungen/IKT_Konferenz_2005_Papers/waelbroeck.pdf

Brandis, G. (2014). *Attorney general opening address. Fair use for the future: A practical look at copyright reform forum*. Australian Digital Alliance. Retrieved from http://www.alrc.gov.au/sites/default/files/pdfs/140214_-_ag_speech_-_ada_copyright_forum_2.pdf

Breaking Bad finale draws record ratings as Australia tops illegal downloads. (2013, October 1). *ABC*. Retrieved from http://www.abc.net.au/news/2013-10-01/breaking-bad-finale-draws-record-ratings-as-australia-tops-ille/4990252

Brown, S. C. (2014). Approaches to digital piracy research: A call for innovation. *Convergence: The International Journal of Research into New Media Technologies*, *20*(2), 129–139.

Burning issue: Anti piracy! (2007, January 1). *FilmInk*. Retrieved from http://www.filmink.com.au/features/burning-issue/

Cairns, L. (2006). *Sapphism on screen: Lesbian desire in french and francophone cinema*. Edinburgh, Scotland: Edinburgh University Press.

Circumventing geo-blocking and online price discrimination. (2013, July 9). *Choice*. Retrieved from http://www. choice.com.au/reviews-and-tests/computers-and-online/networking-and-internet/shopping-online/navigating-online-geoblocks.aspx

Dejean, S. (2009). What can we learn from empirical studies about piracy? *CESifo Economic Studies*, *55*(2), 326–352.

De Vany, A. S., & Walls, W. D. (2007). Estimating the effects of movie piracy on box-office revenue. *Review of Industrial Organization*, *30*(4), 291–301. doi:10.1007/s11151-007-9141-0

Dorling, P. (2013, November 14). Australians may pay the price in Trans-Pacific partnership free trade agreement. *The Sydney Morning Herald*. Retrieved from http://www.smh.com.au/federal-politics/political-news/australians-may-pay-the-price-in-transpacific-partnership-free-trade-agreement-20131113-2xh0m.html

Dwyer, T., & Uricaru, I. (2009). Slashings and subtitles: Romanian media piracy, censorship, and translation. *Velvet Light Trap: A Critical Journal of Film & Television*, *63*, 45–57.

Dyer, R. (1978). Gays in film. *Jump Cut*, 18, 15–16. Retrieved from http://www.ejumpcut.org/archive/onlinessays/JC18folder/GaysinFilmDyer.html

Fitzgerald, S. (2014, March 17). Netflix Canada vs. Netflix USA: What we're missing. *Toronto Sun*. Retrieved from http://www.torontosun.com/2014/03/17/netflix-canada-vs-netflix-usa-what-were-missing

Garrahan, M. (2014, January 9). Digital film sales resuscitate Hollywood revenue stream. *Financial Times*. Retrieved from http://www.ft.com/intl/cms/s/0/0282cc28-78d8-11e3-831c-00144feabdc0.html#axzz3DFP9qAex

Green, B. S. P. (2012, March 28). When stealing isn't stealing. *The* New York *Times*. Retrieved from http://www.nytimes.com/2012/03/29/opinion/theft-law-in-the-21st-century.html?pagewanted=all&_r=

Halliday, J. (2012, August 15). Surfthechannel owner sentenced to four years over piracy. *The Guardian*. Retrieved from http://http://www.theguardian.com/technology/2012/aug/14/anton-vickerman-surfthechannel-sentenced

Hollywood studios lose iiNet download case. (2012, April 20). *ABC Online*. Retrieved from http://www.abc.net.au/news/2012-04-20/iinet-wins-download-case/3962442

Hughes, M. (2014, March 1). 2013 sets all-time box office record. *Forbes*. Retrieved from http://www.forbes.com/sites/markhughes/2014/01/03/2013-sets-all-time-box-office-record

Hutchinson, J. (2014, February 14). Brandis mulls three-strikes rule for internet pirates. *The Australian Financial Review*. Retrieved from http://www.afr.com/p/technology/brandis_mulls_three_strikes_rule_fHbNn5PdCtf5OYW8FeodPO

Jones, J. (Director). (2013). *North Korea: Life inside the secret state* [Documentary]. Channel 4.

Keen, A. (2011, spring). Losing independence. *Directors guild of America*. Retrieved from http://www.dga.org/Craft/DGAQ/All-Articles/1101-Spring-2011/Internet-Theft-Losing-Independence.aspx

Lewis, J. (2007). If you can't protect what you own, you don't own anything: Piracy, privacy, and public relations in 21st century Hollywood. *Cinema Journal*, *46*(2), 145–152.

Lo, M. (2008, May 4). Interview with Zero Chou. *AfterEllen.com*. Retrieved from http://www.afterellen.com/interview-with-zero-chou/05/2008/3

Lobato, R. (2012). *Shadow economies of cinema: Mapping informal film distribution*. London, England: Palgrave Macmillan.

Lobato, R., & Thomas, J. (2012). The business of anti-piracy: New zones of enterprise in the copyright wars. *International Journal of Communication*, *6*, 606–625.

Mick, J. (2011, May 24). U.S. copyright group is now suing nearly 50,000 U.S. citizens for piracy. *DailyTech*. Retrieved from http://www.dailytech.com/US+Copyright+Group+is+Now+Suing+Nearly+50000+US+Citizens+for+Piracy/article21713.html

Moore, C. (2013). Distribution is queen: LGBTQ media on demand. *Cinema Journal*, *53*(1), 137–144.

MPAA. (2013, March). *Theatrical market statistics 2012*. *Motion Picture Association of America*. Retrieved from http://www.mpaa.org/wp-content/uploads/2014/03/2012-Theatrical-Market-Statistics-Report.pdf

Parkes, M. (2013). Making plans for Nigel: The industry trust and film piracy management in the United Kingdom. *Convergence: The International Journal of Research into New Media Technologies*, *19*(1), 25–43.

Pirate website owner gets four years, but what about Google? (2012, August 15). *The Guardian*. Retrieved from http://www.theguardian.com/technology/2012/aug/14/pirate-website-owner-four-years

Russia's Vladimir Putin signs 'anti-gay propaganda' bill into law. (2013, June 30). *ABC Online*. Retrieved from http://www.abc.net.au/news/2013-06-30/russia27s-putin-signs-27anti-gay-propaganda27-bill-into-law/4790498

Sandoval, G. (2010, September 20). Indie filmmakers: Piracy and Google threaten us. *CNET news*. Retrieved from http://news.cnet.com/8301-31001_3-20016920-261.html

Seidler, E. (2010). Dirty money. *Who Profits from Piracy?* [Web page]. Retrieved from www.popuppirates.com

Swan, K. (2007, October 15). *Film industry fights back with anti-piracy campaign*. Retrieved from http://www.abc.net.au/news/2007-10-15/film-industry-fights-back-with-anti-piracy-campaign/698368

Swift, B. (2011, September 10). IPAF begins new anti-piracy campaign, releases consumer research. *Inside Film*. Retrieved from http://if.com.au/2011/09/09/article/IPAF-begins-new-anti-piracy-campaign-releases-consumer-research/YDAKVHMFKT.html

Waterman, D., Ji, S. W., & Rochet, L. R. (2007). Enforcement and control of piracy, copying, and sharing in the movie industry. *Review of Industrial Organization, 30*(4), 255–289.

Weiss, A. (1992). *Vampires & violets: Lesbians in film*. New York, NY: Penguin Books.

Whatling, C. (1997). *Screen dreams: Fantasising lesbians in film*. Manchester, England: Manchester University Press.

White, P. (1999). *Uninvited: Classical Hollywood cinema and lesbian representability*. Bloomington, IN: Indiana University Press.

Wilton, T. (1995). *Immortal, invisible: Lesbians and the moving image*. London, England: Routledge.

Yar, M. (2005). The global 'epidemic' of movie 'piracy': Crime-wave or social construction? *Media, Culture & Society, 27*(5), 677–696.

Yeates, C. (2012, July 13). Why Australian shoppers pay more. *The Sydney Morning Herald*. Retrieved from http://www.smh.com.au/business/why-australian-shoppers-pay-more-20120713-2208v.html

# Anti-Market Research: Piracy, New Media Metrics, and Commodity Communities

Jeremy Wade Morris

*University of Wisconsin-Madison*

Over a decade after Napster's introduction, file sharing programs still shoulder much of the blame for music and other media's declining sales. Although labels and industry associations point their fingers at the harm digital piracy and file-sharing cause, they are less likely to admit the extent to which these anti-markets inform everyday decisions. File-sharing technologies create networks of users that serve as profitable data for ratings and metrics agencies. Using a case study of BigChampagne and its relationship to Napster, this article considers how the look, structure, and function of file-sharing software helped turn an economically threatening community into a commodity and how piracy's disruptive potential is always in tension with processes of commodification.

## INTRODUCTION

Digital piracy, often presented as a bane to the media industries, has been a boon for practices of audience and market research. Even though piracy engenders seemingly disruptive consumptive practices, it contradictorily contributes to the further commodification of new and digital media products. To consider the tension between piracy and commodification, this article provides a case study (Stake, 1994; Yin, 1989) of new media metrics company BigChampagne and its relationship to Napster's original network. It looks at a variety of sources, including a critical textual reading of Napster's interface and key features, an analysis of press articles relating to Napster and BigChampagne, and a political economic investigation of audience measurement strategies. Two questions dominate: 1) Why did Napster present music and connect users in the ways it did? and 2) In what ways do audience measurement practices trouble the narrative of file-sharing as destructive practice? The structure and function of file-sharing software helped turn potentially economically threatening communities of pirates into commodities that could generate revenue and valuable research information. This article adds to the growing literature on file-sharing and piracy by providing a detailed look at the business aspects of Napster, and the ways in which the service and its network contributed to the commodification of digital music. More crucially, this research questions accepted narratives of disruption and looks instead towards the complex layers of innovation, resistance and capture that occur in grey/anti-market spaces. It should be noted that my use of the term "anti-market" is meant to signify the capturing of seemingly disruptive or destructive market practices to further market goals. In this regard, anti-market is similar to

Ramon Laboto's ideas on grey and informal economies and distinct from the term anti-market as used by Fernand Braudel (1982) or Manuel De Landa (1996). The latter scholars describe capitalism as an anti-market since normal market mechanics of supply and demand are significantly distorted by large corporate entities that use monopolization and high levels of concentration and profits to set market standards and conditions rather than respond to existing market ones. Napster users represent an anti-market not because they distort market mechanics, but because they are seemingly placing themselves outside commodity relations by participating in file sharing.

## DISRUPTING THE DISRUPTION

It may seem counter-intuitive that what major labels have vilified as the culprit for declining revenues is one of the prime reasons why a market for digital music exists. Napster brought together a sizeable enough group of users to make the idea of digital music retail viable. Even though Napster may have seemed antithetical to traditional forms of commerce, its own business model was surprisingly similar to other media companies: to gather an audience and sell it to interested companies. Through its software and features, Napster helped build a community that has served as a template not just for other online and new media communities, but for measuring online audiences. Individual Napster users became an analyzable group of listeners and participants that could serve commercial ends. Napster provided a space for an audience that engaged in community-like behaviors, but one that was nonetheless built to be a commodity that would generate sellable data and patterns.

Napster facilitated finding and downloading MP3 files online through its software client and it spread rapidly through fall 1999, with users trading hundreds of thousands of files (Ante, 2000a; Logie, 2006; Taylor, Demont-Heinrich, Broadfoot, Dodge, & Jiana, 2002). By November 1999, the Recording Industry Association of America (RIAA) launched a lawsuit against the company, with prominent musicians filing charges against the service in early 2000 (Sullivan, 1999b). After a series of legal battles, Napster was ordered to shut down in July 2001. Another court stayed that ruling, allowing Napster to remain minimally operational until it filed for bankruptcy in June 2002 (Menn, 2003). The site spent its ensuing years as a relatively unsuccessful subscription service under the management of Roxio and Best Buy. Rhapsody acquired and merged Napster's network with its own in 2011.

Napster thrust piracy into a wider public discussion that has continued as similar services have emerged. Narratives around Napster have either categorized users as revolutionaries or pirates. Many were quick to label Napster's audience as young and deviant even though Napster's software was hardly limited to teens and students (Jones & Lenhart, 2004; Mann, 2000, p. 57; Taylor et al., 2002, pp. 615–616).

Early academic accounts of Napster looked beyond simple claims of piracy to consider the kinds of online community taking place on the service. In line with other work on virtual communities (Rheingold, 1994; Turkle, 1995; Turner, 2005; Wellman, 1999), researchers investigated the bonds formed as users engaged in digital exchange (Giesler & Pohlmann, 2003; Poblocki, 2001). Napster users identified with creator Shawn Fanning as a young tech-savvy "revolutionary" and saw Napster not just as an application for sharing but also as a tool of protest against inflated album and ticket prices and a broader regime of intellectual property (Taylor et al., 2002, p. 616). Napster was a transient space, a "temporary hypercommunity" (Kozinets, 2002) where users were engaging in radical acts of civil disobedience, and practicing divergent social and economic logics that might remove them from traditional market relations (Barbrook, 2002; Giesler & Pohlmann, 2003; Kozinets, 2002; Leyshon, 2003).

This conception of Napster users as a community of rebellious downloaders and piracy as a radical social act is appealing, and has persisted as newer services have emerged. However, it conveniently ignores the control music labels and industry associations have over the flow of copyrighted materials (McCourt & Burkart, 2003). It also overlooks the fact that the program's user base did not arise spontaneously around a piece of software. It was planned, managed and cultivated by Napster. Napster had a corporate structure, venture capitalist investors, business development managers, and lawyers (Menn, 2003). As much as Napster users were exploring "new forms of social exchanges and cooperation" (Beuscart, 2005, p. 2), they were also a key resource for potential profits. Napster users may have individually engaged in disruptive, anti-commercial behavior by sharing files but, collectively, they played a commercial role by gathering around the software in ways that allowed for the further monitoring, measuring and commodification of digital music and its audiences.

While few articles investigated Napster's corporate motives (Ante, 2000a, 2000b; Sullivan, 1999a; Varanini, 2000), much of the company's business strategies and documents were never made public early on (Menn, 2003, p. 1). The legal and cultural issues the program sparked were of primary interest. Only by ignoring Napster's commercial nature could it be heralded as a revolution and a threat to private property and capitalism (Dean, 2005, p. 62).

Napster's role in the rise of everyday piracy and the decline of the value of music and media goes far beyond simple disruption. The increasing prevalence of file sharing and communities that have formed around the issues sparked by digital piracy have certainly brought challenges to traditional forms of content circulation and commodification. They have also brought new and potentially problematic means of muting these challenges, hinting at a much more complicated relationship that piracy and file-sharing play in the making, marketing and distribution of media products.

## ORGANIZING THE DISORGANIZED

Understanding Napster users as a community, but one that was planned and managed, helps us reconsider the audiences "pirate" services gather. Smythe (1981) argued that what media ultimately produce is an audience commodity. Audiences work for broadcasters as they consume media content; they are packaged as commodities broadcasters sell to advertisers. Smythe's work has been criticized, reworked and updated, with more attention paid to the role ratings companies play in constructing audiences (Meehan, 2001, p. 215). Media metrics companies are as much manufacturing companies as they are measurement ones (Bermejo, 2009, p. 138; Miller, 1994). Rather than reporting any kind of true total viewing audience, ratings companies provide what Napoli (2011), building on Ettma and Whitney (1994), has called the institutionally effective audience: those that can be efficiently integrated into the economics of media industries.

New media extend and complicate this measurement/manufacturing process. New media and the Internet make possible different ways of assembling audiences as workers (Arvidsson & Colleoni, 2012; Bruns, 2006; Fuchs, 2010). As users play an increasing role in providing the content for sites, the line between audiences as laboring viewers or listeners and audiences as creators or producers blurs (Coté & Pybus, 2007). The commodification of user content and communication creates what Jakobsson and Stiernstedt call "platform economics," where Web 2.0 services and other such sites put the products of the cultural commons in service of economic profit (2010, 2012). These economic models both foster and depend upon various levels of audience labor, creating spaces in which complicated networks of sociality, connectivity and economic activity combine (van Dijck, 2009, 2011). As Bolin suggests, audiences perform two kinds of work. First, a user produces identities and meanings from media, either for themselves or for others. Second, the objectified forms of these meanings are then made into a product for further consumption by media industries (2012, pp. 797–798). Web 2.0's supposed innovation of participatory media must also be viewed as fundamental to new and emerging business models. As van Dijck notes, "social values such as popularity, attention, and connectivity [. . .] are impalpably translated into monetary values and redressed in business models made possible by digital technology" (2011, p. 3).

New media also allow for different means of measuring and representing audiences. There are more tools than ever for advertisers or producers to track consumer behavior. However, audience fragmentation and added audience agency through new technologies and formats have made predicting audience patterns more slippery. Any audience is a balance between predicted, measured and actual audiences (Napoli, 2001, p. 66). As the gap between measured and actual audience widens and traditional ad-supported models become less effective, new media companies have found other ways to extract value from users, "such as audience members' personal data, research services, and various cross-promotional opportunities" (Napoli, 2001, p. 71). New media producers rely increasingly on cybernetic commodities, that is, on the ability to sell data about users of entertainment commodities rather than the sale of those commodities directly (Andrejevic, 2007; Mosco, 1996). The act of being watched becomes as valuable as watching advertisements was formerly.

For over two decades, the music industries have relied on Nielsen's SoundScan and BroadcastDataSystem (BDS) technologies, and the Billboard charts they help produce, to gauge sales and artist popularity. New media and new consumption habits trouble these traditional tactics, though, given that estimates suggest between 75% and 90% of all music obtained in many markets is unlicensed (International Federation of the Phonographic Industry, 2009, 2012; RIAA). While Nielsen has recently expanded its measurement data to include digital sales, online streams, YouTube videos, and social network plays, it was slow to do so, and it remains wedded to the correlation of popularity and sales—despite the fact that a good deal of music circulation occurs outside traditional realms.

Although file-sharing services helped widen the gap between measured and actual audiences, these same technologies open up new forms of measurement and monitoring. Andrejevic uses the term "digital enclosure" to suggest how new media technologies have a tendency to create an ecosystem that promotes added interactivity for users but depends highly on users surrendering personal information to heavily monitored databases (2007, p. 2). As anti-corporate as its image appeared, Napster was a prototypical version of a digital enclosure. Napster's networked nature and the amount of information that circulated through it provided a highly useable database. Although Napster intended to use this data itself (Menn, 2003, p. 122), its legal troubles prevented it. Instead, other companies looking to leech off of Napster emerged to use this cybernetic information (Brown, 2001). In doing so, they put pirate practices to work in service of commodification and helped lay the foundation for practices and techniques that have become central.

Perhaps most interesting in the case of Napster is that most of its users were working to remove themselves from the institutionally effective audience by avoiding the typical reporting statistics that accompany music commodity purchases. Napster's audience became a test case for how to account for what had previously been unaccountable and how to put that accounting in the service of further commodification. Even though Napster may not have profited directly from its audience, the community it brought together presented novel and conflicting opportunities for advertising, market research and surveillance (McCourt & Burkart, 2003, pp. 335, 343). Napster users may have disrupted the institutionally effective audience, but they were key to spurring new media measurement techniques that continue to occupy a central, if silent, place in media and cultural industries.

## MEASURING THE IMMEASURABLE

The increasing gap between actual and perceived audience is part of what drove the emergence of a new breed of music measurement companies. As a growing amount of musical content moved online, and consumers started using sanctioned and unsanctioned services to access that content, a host of companies developed metrics to measure this slippage and fragmentation of the institutionally effective audience. These emerging services sought to fill a similar function as SoundScan, but they borrowed tools and tactics from the burgeoning online advertising and audience research sector. This sector, according to Bermejo, exploded in the mid to late 1990s as an array of companies and research services began measuring/manufacturing an online audience product, usually tracked through logfiles, tags and other traces of audience activity (2009, p. 143). The music metric companies that emerged in the late 1990s and early 2000s applied these intelligence strategies to tracking the circulation of music and tried to sell resulting data back to interested parties. Though their services are still relatively under-publicized, companies like BigChampagne work at providing comprehensive online audience measurement and brand management tools for labels. These information intermediaries play an important role in both producing audiences and mitigating risk in the cultural industries, but they do so using data from sources that are dismissed and decried by the industry.

Given that BigChampagne is one of the best known and most used new media audience measurement companies, it deserves special focus. Officially founded in 2000, its earliest services involved providing data and charts about the files that users were trading most frequently on file sharing networks (Howe, 2003). The company was regularly cited as an authority in tech and popular press reports on file sharing throughout the early 2000s. Although the company emphasizes file sharing less as its primary source of data, BigChampagne continues to provide charts, trend-watching prediction, and music intelligence services by compiling data from digital music retail outlets, social networks, web portals, and file sharing services. In 2011, Live Nation acquired BigChampagne, giving the latter access to a huge database of event, ticketing and merchandising, and other "offline" data. BigChampagne's tagline "Now You Know Everything" hints both at the promise they offer clients, and the promise new technologies offer for audience measurement (BigChampagne, 2010).

However, BigChampagne's reputation as the "Nielsen Ratings of the peer-to-peer world" (Howe, 2003) is not the primary reason to focus on it. Rather, it is because of the service's early relationship with, and continued debt to, Napster. Before BigChampagne started tracking file sharing traffic, the company's founder, Eric Garland, was using Napster as tool for direct marketing. Napster's architecture allowed users to see which songs users were downloading, so Garland built programs that sent direct messages to users through Napster's chat feature (Howe, 2003). A promotion for songwriter Aimee Mann, for example, sent downloaders a message saying: "I see you have some Aimee Mann songs on your hard drive. Aimee Mann has a new promotional song, go check it out at aimeemann.com" (Brown, 2001). The promotion resulted in 1,700 new members joining Mann's mailing list (Brown, 2001). Despite additional successes, other artists and record companies were hesitant to work with Garland and BigChampagne. The record labels were especially reticent about promoting any legitimate use of peer-to-peer technology and contradicting their no-tolerance policy towards file sharing networks (Brown, 2001). If companies dealt with BigChampagne during the early and mid 2000s, it was in secret (Howe, 2003).

However, as file sharing networks proliferated and as the amount of data generated from file-sharers increased, many of the major labels started using BigChampagne's information to supplement campaigns. Documented campaigns include Capitol Records consulting with them for marketing Radiohead's *Amnesiac*, Led Zeppelin using their data to craft their reunion concert setlist in 2007, and My Chemical Romance relying on the company to choose singles from their 2004 album (Lange, 2009; Mathews, 2001). Garland claims the company's sophisticated data collection techniques—which have led to partnerships with Clear Channel, Billboard Radio Monitor, and other traditional media outlets—come from the fact that "P2P [. . .] allows a singular opportunity to observe really intimate consumer behavior. You're not asking them what's your taste in music, games, books, what have you – you're looking in the pantry, straight into the fridge" (Garland, as cited in Brown, 2001).

This intimate view comes not just from BigChampagne's technology but also from the interfaces and infrastructures of technologies like Napster. Through these file-sharing programs, BigChampagne can participate directly in BitTorrent swarms and monitor trackers ceaselessly. They can collect information about files uploaded and downloaded in real time and determine what's "popular" through IP addresses, claiming to be better than 99% accurate at a country level and slightly less at the city level (E. Garland, personal communication, August 6, 2009). BigChampagne's software is an overlay on top of all this activity, capable of recording and archiving the contents list of shared folders and p2p search queries. For BigChampagne and other market research firms, these connected and visible networks are like "gold mines" of data (Olsen, 2001). They are also a way to turn a community of file sharers into cybernetic commodity. While traditional ratings companies typically set out to track the institutionally effective and commercially relevant audiences, BigChampagne built their business on tracking those who thought they had removed themselves from it.

## COMMODIFYING THE COMMUNITY

Rather than a traditional audience commodity, Napster is closer to what Fry (1977) describes as a "commodity community": an audience that is very much a community, but one that was built and maintained as such in order to serve as a commodity. Fry coins the term in a study about neighborhoods and residential units that are "intentionally planned, designed, and developed as an economic endeavour" (1977, p. 116). In these pre-conceived communities, residential units are sold in conjunction with a "'way of life,' culture, and social organization which is an implicit, if not an explicit part of the deal" (Fry, 1977, p. 116). Commodity communities rely on the culture of the community to attract interest, either from homebuyers or from those looking to invest in or extract value from the community. Through design of the environmental space and economic control of resources, community developers must convince buyers and sellers of the type of community they hope to create. Commodity communities depend on a fairly long-term and structural involvement of those managing them. Community developers are constantly shaping and trimming the community's features in order to enhance its culture and values (Fry, 1977).

Early on, the people behind Napster had a vision of the role its users would play. Through its business plans, software, website and marketing, Napster designed a program conducive to creating community that could provide value and profit (Menn, 2003, p. 102). Napster tried to build this community through discursive and technical means. From explicit mission statements on its website—"Welcome to Napster, the future of music. [. . .] By creating a virtual community, Napster ensures a vast collection of MP3s for download" (Napster, 1999)—to encouraging users to show support by writing to major record labels and the RIAA during its legal troubles (Napster, 2000), Napster called on its community and hoped to use them as a resource for garnering public support and for tactical activism.

Napster's discursive attempts at community building were ultimately less successful than their technical innovations. Napster was built on Fanning's desire to have "a real-time index that reflects all sites that are up and available to others on the network at that moment" (Fanning, as cited in Menn, 2003, p. 34). This meant that Napster, like many of today's instant messenger clients or social networks, provided a constant awareness of the presence of other users and of the contents of the network. Napster's near instantaneous indexing of all the files on the system meant that as each user logged on, their shared folder was visible to other users on the system. By focusing on the vast amount of material in circulation, the interface heightened the affective experience of searching for and finding music. Each file query was an indication both of the amount of movement taking place on the network as well as the sizeable amount of other users who were engaged in a shared practice. Searching simultaneously revealed the music users were seeking and validated participation in the community.

In addition to indicating the availability of songs, searches returned other information about the file such as bit rate, usernames, and details about their connection speeds. While this information seems like minor technical details, the choice to include this metadata was one of the ways that Napster brought its commodity community together. It allowed users and companies like BigChampagne to peer into the lives and habits of other users as they browsed or traded. To know that "dsknutz" had a T1 connection meant knowing that your download would be served quickly but it also set up a series of inferences about a user within the community. Metadata of this nature was displayed in the transfer window, giving users and companies like BigChampagne measurements for which files were popular with which users.

Napster also included community-oriented features such as Chat and HotList to help organize its audience. The Chat feature let users maintain loose ties on the network either individually or through chat rooms. The HotList, on the other hand, allowed users to compile a list of peers to "follow." Each time hot listed peers signed on, the contents of their library became visible to followers. Like the chat function, the HotList facilitated more targeted searching, and focused users on the rest of the Napster community. These features were ways of following users with particular tastes and primitive forms of more complex music recommendation systems currently available. They were a way of weeding through the massive amount of music on the network.

By integrating the choices of other users into one's own music search process through the Chat and Hot List features, Napster's interface facilitated the age-old practice of sharing music and telling other people about it, enabling not just the movement of music but also the movement of discourses about music (Jones, 2002, pp. 214, 225).

These features were instrumental for gathering and organizing Napster's commodity community. They made visible the idea of swapping music and brought together disparate and transient users with hard drives full of music and connected them in ways that shaped how users came to understand the act of file sharing. They provided the glue for building the commodity community. In these respects, Napster's primary innovation was more organizational than technical (Beuscart, 2005). Napster's main achievement was how it organized its user base through its software's features and interface. While Napster's messaging through its website was an overt attempt to build/facilitate a community, the interface worked at a more subtle level. It drew users together in a series of technical and social relationships—relationships that were premised on the circulation of files and the making visible to other users that movement and connection.

The same technical features that helped assemble this community also helped companies like BigChampagne commodify it. They provided near real-time access to the number of files being traded, the height and by-region popularity of certain artists and songs, and a host of technical and social information that could be extracted via the connections between users logged into Napster. The commodity community invites a multitude of relationships, whether social or commercial in nature. Napster's audience may have logged on for the free music or for social engagement, but in the process they offered up a host of data for other actors on the network, giving companies like BigChampagne, and its clients, greater insight into user behaviors and preferences than ever before. It is precisely this point about Napster and file sharing networks that often gets buried under narratives about digital pirates or youthful revolution against an out of touch industry: Napster's software disrupted some traditional industrial practices and intensified others.

## RATIONALIZING THE IRRATIONAL

Like SoundScan data and BDS information, BigChampagne and other such services serve a rhetorical function. They justify decisions on which acts to invest in and they provide evidence of popularity to labels and promotional companies that have spent millions to achieve that. They rationalize risk in essentially irrational industries, though they do so by promising a level of granularity that older forms of media measurement could not deliver. New media metrics companies like BigChampagne raise alarm about an industrial problem and simultaneously provide a solution. They are a reflection of an industry struggling to adjust to digitization while negotiating their relationship with disruptive technologies. They are also an indication that as much as file sharing is positioned as piracy, the unsanctioned circulation of media commodities is still a generative practice. Through BigChampagne and other such companies, record labels and other media companies have found multiple ways to profit and learn from the commodity communities the various anti-market spaces and technologies piracy enables.

In his book on the distribution of film in the digital age, Lobato uses the term "shadow economies of cinema" to describe the informal, unmeasured, and unregulated circulation of audiovisual goods that has become an increasingly central aspect of cinematic commerce and culture (2012, p. 40). Although his analysis is trained specifically on the vast infrastructure that supports pirate and other informal networks—an infrastructure that overlaps with the one supporting unsanctioned circulation of music—more interesting is the "slippery" distinction he sees between shadowy and legitimate practices (2012, p. 41). For Lobato, "there is a great deal of traffic between the formal and the informal over time and space" and that, in many ways, formal distribution and production channels often rely on informal ones for products, information and profit (2012, p. 41). The resulting grey economies are neither cleanly formal nor informal.

Although the practices of online audience measurement do not begin with BigChampagne and Napster, the assemblage of those two services stands out as a model for how audience measurement practices could no longer be based solely on institutionally effective audiences. To measure the audience fully, tools that could measure both industrially sanctioned and unsanctioned behaviors needed to be developed. BigChampagne's early use of cybernetic data has served as a template for a host of similar music and media measurement companies. Beyond music, we can look to other recent examples, like when Australian broadcasting media giant Fairfax listed the monitoring of BitTorrent as one of its key strategies for acquiring new content for its television line-up (Ernesto, 2010).

These firms are related to the more general sector of companies, such as Radian 6 or Sysomos, that provide "sentiment analysis" by monitoring all kinds of signals and cues from social media and other networked audiences (Hearn, 2010; Pang & Lee, 2008). This burgeoning industry of infomediaries uses new technologies and the highly interactive current media environment to monitor, to participate in, and to guide online feedback about an entertainment property. They look beyond measurements of exposure and sales—what SoundScan or BDS typically measure— and promise insight into intimate mindsets such as "engagement," "attention," or "anticipation." They do so through formal and informal channels and specialize in trying to capture intimate and affective consumer activities (Hearn, 2010). Garland's comment about looking straight into the file sharer's fridge to gain access to pure action rather than discourse about action speaks to the infomediary-promoted promise that new technologies and a highly interactive media environment provide novel traces of the audience's behaviors and emotional responses that can be tracked, compiled, analyzed, processed, and sold.

The relationship between file sharing technologies, piracy and media metrics agencies speaks to the commodification of the cybernetic layer of information surrounding music, but it also underscores the hazy relationship between sanctioned and unsanctioned economic activity within various media industries (Lobato, 2012). Although denounced as an anti-market, file sharing networks offer a substantial amount of consumer information for those who know how to collect, to measure and to analyze it. These data-mining practices trouble the standard narrative surrounding file sharing's effects on the music industries. This opportunistic use of unsanctioned practices is not limited to file sharing. There are related cases, such as when event companies like Live Nation sell blocks of tickets to scalpers (Cloonan, 2012). Although promoters and labels frown publicly at the practice, this secondary market helps drive down availability of tickets and drive up prices, ultimately benefitting promoters (Cloonan, 2012). There is also the case of video game publishers who discourage modification of their software publicly, but privately incorporate the unauthorized hacks and modifications in order to re-sell those innovations (de Peuter & Dyer-Witherford, 2005). As with the metrics extracted from file sharing networks, these cases all involve market spaces and practices that are officially condemned but unofficially add significant value to the production process. Even though users of file sharing networks were engaging in seemingly disruptive consumptive practices, they were nevertheless contributing to further commodification of new media products. Not only was Napster a business, but it was one that, despite public protestations from major labels and industry associations, showed media industries the wealth of consumer insights and data that could be gleaned from commodity communities.

The challenges piracy has posed to the media industries are substantial, but not all those changes have turned out to be as disruptive as early discourses around file-sharing technologies suggested. File sharing has proven to be, as Andersson Schwarz suggests, both "uncontrollable and unyielding, as well as compliant and business friendly" (2014, p. 1). As new streaming services emerge that offer a wide catalogue of music for a low monthly subscription fee or for free with ad-supported listening, there will be increasing pressure to mine and to make use of user data. Given the number of paid versus unpaid subscribers on many of these services, these sites must make up for their lack of revenue by monetizing data gleaned from users. Spotify has around 40 million users. 10 million are paying subscribers (Spotify, 2014). While Spotify promotes its model by arguing that it is shifting users away from file sharing networks to a paid service, this logic belies the larger fact that the very rise of streaming services depends highly on the existence and utility of a commodity community. In this light, the conjuncture of Napster and BigChampagne stands out as a prototypical template for the business models on which many of these new services are now based.

Far from being a rogue piece of software that destroyed the music business and turned everyday consumers into plundering pirates, Napster's early version was a business that helped create a market for digital music commodities and served as a model for how new media properties manage affective and economic relationships with their users. These users and their interactions have become key metrics for digital market analysts and new media metrics companies; an entire subindustry of infomediaries now depend on these data and sell the data back to the very companies that publicly crusade against the legality of such technologies and services. Old business models may be becoming obsolete, but the new business models emerging in their place benefit both new and old players in the music industries as they take advantage of novel ways to capture the digital consumer. Although mining data from file-sharing and other practices deemed piratical by record labels and other music industry firms remains a research strategy that "dare not speak its name" (Howe, 2003), it is a strategy that continues to speak to the conflicting notions of piracy as social change and as commodified practice.

## FUNDING

This research was funded in part by the University of Wisconsin-Madison's Graduate Studies Fall Research Competition.

## REFERENCES

Andersson Schwarz, J. (2014). *Online file sharing: Innovations in media consumption.* New York, NY: Routledge.

Andrejevic, M. (2007). *iSpy: Surveillance and power in the interactive era.* Lawrence, KS: University Press of Kansas.

Ante, S. (2000a, August 14). *Inside Napster.* Retrieved from http://www.businessweek.com/stories/2000-08-13/inside-napster

Ante, S. (2000b, April 12). *Napster's Shawn Fanning: The teen who woke up web music.* Retrieved from http://www.businessweek.com/ebiz/0004/em0412.htm

Arvidsson, A., & Colleoni, E. (2012). Value in informational capitalism and on the internet. *The Information Society*, *28*(3), 135–150. doi:10.1080/01972243.2012.669449

Barbrook, R. (2002). The Napsterisation of everything. *Science as Culture*, *2*(11), 277–285.

Bermejo, F. (2009). Audience manufacture in historical perspective: From broadcasting to Google. *New Media & Society*, *11*(1–2), 133–154. doi:10.1177/1461444808099579

Beuscart, J. S. (2005). Napster users between community and clientele: The formation and regulation of a sociotechnical group. *Sociologie Du Travail*, *47*, S1–16. doi:doi:10.1016/j.soctra.2005.08.003

BigChampagne. (2010). *BigChampagne: Company overview (company profile)*. Retrieved from http://investing.businessweek.com/research/stocks/private/snapshot.asp?privcapId=7701315

Bolin, G. (2012). The labour of media use. *Information, Communication & Society*, *15*(6), 796–814. doi:10.1080/1369118x.2012.677052

Braudel, F. (1982). *Civilization and capitalism, 15th-18th century. vol. 2*. New York, NY: Harper and Row.

Brown, J. (2001). *The Napster parasites*. Retrieved from http://archive.salon.com/tech/feature/2001/02/09/napster_parasites/

Bruns, A. (2006, June 28–July 1). *Towards produsage: Futures for user-led content production*. Paper presented at the Cultural Attitudes towards Communication and Technology, Tartu, Estonia.

Burkart, P. (2010). *Music and cyberliberties*. Middletown, CT: Wesleyan University Press.

Cloonan, M. (2012). *Mastering tickets*. Retrieved from http://livemusicexchange.org/blog/mastering-tickets/

Coté, M., & Pybus, J. (2007). Learning to immaterial labour 2.0: MySpace and social networks *Ephemera*, *7*(1), 88–106.

de Peuter, G., & Dyer-Witherford, N. (2005). *Games of empire: Global capitalism and video games*. Minneapolis, MN: University of Minnesota Press.

Dean, J. (2005). Communicative capitalism: Circulation and the foreclosure of politics. *Cultural Politics*, *1*(1), 51–74. doi:10.2752/174321905778054845

De Landa, M. (1996). Markets and antimarkets in a world economy. In S. Aronowitz, B. Martinsons, & M. Menser (Eds.), *Technoscience and cyberculture* (pp. 181–194). New York, NY: Routledge.

Ernesto. (2010). *Show doing well on BitTorrent? We'll buy it, says media giant*. Retrieved from http://torrentfreak.com/show-doing-well-on-bittorrent-well-buy-it-121010/

Ettema, J., & Whitney, C. (1994). The money arrow: An introduction to audiencemaking. In J. Ettema & C. Whitney (Eds.), *Audiencemaking: How the media create the audience* (pp. 1–18). Thousand Oaks, CA: Sage.

Fry, C. (1977). The community as a commodity: The age graded case. *Human Organization*, *36*(2), 115–123.

Fuchs, C. (2010). Labor in informational capitalism and on the internet. *The Information Society*, *26*(3), 179–196. doi:10.1080/01972241003712215

Garfinkel, S., & Cox, D. (2009). *Finding and archiving the internet footprint*. Paper presented at the First Digital Lives Research Conference: Personal Digital Archives for the 21st Century, London, England.

Garnham, N. (2001). Contribution to a political economy of mass-communication [1986]. In M. G. Durham & D. M. Kellner (Eds.), *Media and cultural studies: Keywords* (pp. 225–252). Oxford, England: Blackwell.

Giesler, M., & Pohlmann, M. (2003). The social form of Napster: Cultivating the paradox of consumer emancipation. *Advances in Consumer Research*, *30*, 94–100.

Gitelman, L. (2006). *Always already new: Media, history and the data of culture*. Cambridge, MA: MIT Press.

Hearn, A. (2010). Structuring feeling: Web 2.0, online ranking and rating, and the digital 'reputation' economy. *Ephemera*, *10*(3/4), 421–438. http://www.ephemeraweb.org/journal/10-3/10-3ephemeranov10.pdf-page=212

Howe, J. (2003). BigChampagne is watching you. *Wired, 11.*

International Federation of the Phonographic Industry. (2009). *Digital music report 2009: New business models for a changing environment*. London, England: Author.

IFPI. (2012). *Digital music report 2012: Expanding choice. Going global*. London, England: Author.

Jakobsson, P., & Stiernstedt, F. (2010). Pirates of silicon valley: State of exception and dispossession in Web 2.0. *First Monday*, *15*(7).

Jakobsson, P., & Stiernstedt, F. (2012). Reinforcing property by strengthening the commons: A new media policy paradigm? *Triple C: Cognition, Communication, Cooperation*, *10*(1), 49–55.

Jones, S. (2002). Music that moves: Popular music, distribution and network technologies. *Cultural Studies*, *16*(2), 213–232. doi:10.1080/09502380110107562

Jones, S., & Lenhart, A. (2004). Music downloading and listening: Findings from the pew internet and American life project. *Popular Music and Society*, *27*(2), 185–199. doi:10.1080/03007760410001685822

Kozinets, R. V. (2002). Can consumers escape the market? Emancipatory illuminations from burning man. *Journal of Consumer Research, 29*. doi:10.1086/339919

Lange, D. (2009, October 16). Taking music risks. Retrieved from http://mcvaymediarocks.blogspot.com/2009/10/taking-music-risks.html

Leyshon, A. (2003). Scary monsters: Free software, peer-to-peer networks and the spectre of the gift. *Environment and Planning D: Society and Space, 21*(5), 533–558. doi:10.1068/d48j

Lobato, R. (2012). *Shadow economies of cinema: Mapping informal film distribution*. London, England: Palgrave.

Logie, J. (2006). *Peers, pirates, and persuasion: Rhetoric in the peer-to-peer debates*. Anderson, SC: Parlor Press.

Mann, C. C. (2000, September). The Heavenly Jukebox. *The Atlantic, 286*, 39–59.

Mathews, A. W. (2001, October 29). Applause, applause: What do audiences want? Entertainment companies are looking for answers on the web. *The Wall Street Journal*, p. R.8.

McCourt, T., & Burkart, P. (2003). When creators, corporations and consumers collide: Napster and the development of on-line music distribution. *Media, Culture and Society, 25*(3), 333–350. doi:10.1177/0163443703025003003

McCourt, T., & Rothenbuhler, E. W. (1997). Soundscan and the consolidation of control. *Media, Culture & Society, 19*(2), 201–218. doi:10.1177/016344397019002005

Meehan, E. (1984). Ratings and the institutional approach: A third answer to the commodity question. *Critical Studies in Mass Communication, 1*(2), 216–225.

Meehan, E. (2001). Gendering the commodity audience: Critical media research, feminism and political economy. In E. Meehan & E. Riordan (Eds.), *Sex & Money* (pp. 209–222). Minneapolis, MN: University of Minnesota Press.

Menn, J. (2003). *All the rave: The rise and fall of Shawn Fanning's Napster*. New York, NY: Crown Business.

Miller, P. (1994). Made-to-order and standardized audiences: Forms of reality in audience measurement. In J. Ettema & C. Whitney (Eds.), *Audiencemaking: How the media create the audience* (pp. 57–74). Thousand Oaks, CA: Sage.

Mosco, V. (1996). *The political economy of communication: Rethinking and renewal*. Thousand Oaks, CA: Sage.

Murdock, G. (1978). Blindspots about western Marxism: A reply to Dallas Smythe. *Canadian Journal of Political and Social Theory, 2*(2), 109–119.

Murphy, J., Hashim, N. H., & O'Connor, P. (2007). Take me back: Validating the wayback machine. *Journal of Computer-Mediated Communication, 13*(1).

Napoli, P. M. (2001). The Audience product and the new media environment: Implications for the economics of media industries. *The International Journal on Media Management, 3*(2), 66–73. doi:10.1080/14241270109389949

Napoli, P. M. (2011). *Audience evolution: New technologies and the transformation of media audiences*. New York, NY: Columbia University Press.

Napster. (1999, October 8). It's here: Napster v2.0 is now available. Retrieved from http://web.archive.org/web/19991008215720/http://napster.com/

Napster. (2000, August 15). Support Napster! Retrieved from http://web.archive.org/web/20000815053013/http://www.napster.com/

Olsen, S. (2001). Will instant messaging become instant spamming? Retrieved from http://news.cnet.com/2100-1023-252765.html

Pang, B., & Lee, L. (2008). Opinion mining and sentiment analysis. *Foundations and Trends in Information Retrieval, 21*(1–2), 1–135. doi:10.1561/1500000011

Poblocki, K. (2001). The Napster network community. *First Monday, 6*(11). doi:10.5210%2Ffm.v6i11.899

Rheingold, H. (1994). *The virtual community: Homesteading on the electronic frontier*. New York, NY: HarperPerennial.

RIAA. RIAA homepage: Anti-piracy. Retrieved from http://www.riaa.com/issues/piracy/default.asp

Robinson, L., & Halle, D. (2002). Digitization, the internet, and the arts: eBay, Napster, SAG and e-books. *Qualitative Sociology, 25*(3), 359–383. doi:10.1023/A:1016034013716

Sernoe, J. (2005). Now we're on the top, top of the pops: The performance of non mainstream music on Billboard's albums charts, 1981–2001. *Popular Music and Society, 28*(5), 639–662. doi:10.1080/03007760500142670

Smythe, D. W. (1981). On the audience commodity and its work. In M. G. Durham & D. Kellner (Eds.), *Media and Cultural Studies: Keywords* (pp. 253–279). Oxford, England: Blackwell.

Spitz, D., & Hunter, S. D. (2005). Contested codes: The social construction of Napster. *The Information Society, 21*, 169–180. doi:10.1080/01972240490951890

Spotify. (2014). Spotify hits 10 million global subscribers? Retrieved from https://press.spotify.com/int/2014/05/21/spotify-hits-10-million-global-subscribers/

Stake, R. E. (1994). Case studies. In N. K. Denzin & Y. S. Lincoln (Eds.), *Handbook of qualitative research* (pp. 236–247). Thousand Oaks, CA: Sage.

Sullivan, J. (1999a, November 1). Napster: Music is for sharing. Retrieved from http://www.wired.com/print/science/discoveries/news/1999/11/32151

Sullivan, J. (1999b, November 15). RIAA suing upstart startup. Retrieved from http://www.wired.com/techbiz/media/news/1999/11/32559

Taylor, B. C., Demont-Heinrich, C., Broadfoot, K. J., Dodge, J., & Jiana, C. (2002). New media and the circuit of cyber culture: Conceptualizing Napster. *Journal of Broadcasting and Electronic Media*, *46*(4), 607–629. doi:10.1207/s15506878jobem4604_7

Turkle, S. (1995). *Life on the screen: Identity in the age of the internet*. New York, NY: Simon & Schuster.

Turner, F. (2005). Where the counterculture met the new economy: The well and the origins of virtual community. *Technology and Culture*, *46*, 485–512. doi:10.1353/tech.2005.0154

van Dijck, J. (2009). Users like you? Theorizing agency in user-generated content. *Media, Culture & Society*, *31*(1), 41–58.

van Dijck, J. (2011). Facebook as a tool for producing sociality and connectivity. *Television & New Media*, *13*(2), 160–176. doi:10.1177/1527476411415291

Varanini, G. (2000, March 3). Q&A: Napster creator Shawn Fanning. Retrieved from http://www.zdnet.com/news/q-a-napster-creator-shawn-fanning/96066

Wellman, B. (1999). *Networks in the global village: Life in contemporary communities*. Boulder, CO: Westview Press.

Yin, R. K. (1989). *Case study research: Design and methods, vol. 5*. London, England: Sage.

# The Piratical Ethos in Streams of Language

Justin Lewis

*Western Oregon University*

This article conducts a discourse analysis related to intellectual property gathered from digital piracy communities. By conducting a quantitative analysis of qualitative data, it renders an account of the piratical subject by exploring what Andersson Schwarz calls "specimens of reasoning" concerning intellectual property and piracy. Varying attitudes toward intellectual property are produced from the data. The outputs of this analysis challenge mainstream articulations of piratical motivations, drawing attention to the complex and often contradictory attitudes that pirates evince with respect to intellectual property. Attention is paid to attitudes that convey support of and resistance to intellectual property on technological, social, and economic grounds.

## INTRODUCTION

Since the spread of digital media in the early 1990s, debates over the politics and cultures of internet piracy have greatly increased in number, extending into popular and academic discourses in legal (Boyle, 1997; Cohen, 2012; Halbert, 2005; Rose, 1993; Vaidhyanathan, 2001; Woodmansee, 1994), humanistic (DeVoss & Porter, 2006; Hawk, 2012; Kennedy & Howard, 2013; Logie, 2006; Reyman, 2010), and cultural domains (Barlow, 1994; Doctorow, 2008; Lessig, 2008). The convenient division tends toward a structuring binary: copyleft versus copyright. This accommodating dyad pits a civic, participatory, and democratic digital culture against the protectionist, capitalist, and corporatized world of Big Media. Salvos in this war revolve around consumer ability to circulate, distribute, consume, and reproduce media and culture inside anachronistic intellectual property regimes conceived in an analog era. At the center one finds the pirate, a subject both lauded and ridiculed for acts of appropriation, theft, and redistribution (Cummings, 2013; Johns, 2011; Mason, 2009; Strangelove, 2005).

The power of the copyleft versus copyright binary is remarkable; so much so that mainstream arguments against and for intellectual property define pirates before pirates are able to define themselves. For the copyleft, arguments against the intensification of intellectual property are rooted in liberal humanist theories of utilitarianism and the public domain. These stances elevate enclosure and ecology as fundamental metaphors for understanding the danger posed by overreaching intellectual property protections (Boyle, 1997, 2003; Logie, 2006; Vaidhyanathan, 2001). Conversely, the copyright finds their footing in Enlightenment articulations of the "sweat

---

Color versions of one or more of the figures in the article can be found online at http://www.tandfonline.com/hppc.

of the brow" (Locke, 1980) as well as Romantic notions of authorial genius (Biagioli, 2011; Young, 1966).

The enduring rhetorical power of Enlightenment tensions between self and other structure the digital copyright debate; however, few studies have invited pirates to speak for themselves concerning their attitudes and ideologies toward intellectual property, copyright and piracy. Notable exceptions include scholarship on internet and piracy studies from Sweden and Germany. Lindgren (2012, 2013), Andersson Schwarz (2012, 2015), and Andersson Schwarz and Larsson (2013) make strides toward understanding the modes of reasoning file-sharers use to justify their practice *ex post facto* and provide evidence that structuring binaries such as private versus public, corporate versus community, or copyleft versus copyright do not particularly help us understand the "copyfight." This dearth of firsthand research suggests one of two things—*either* pirates evince the positions to the issue proffered by the copyleft-copyright *or* few researchers outside of Sweden and Germany have bothered to ask pirates about their perspectives. To discover piratical motivation and piratical ideology, this research project rejects *a priori* justifications for or against intellectual property protections, instead approaching pirates in their own words. Following a grounded theoretic process of analytic induction (Geisler, 2004), this study quantifies qualitative streams of piratical language to uncover the motivations, ideologies, and attitudes toward intellectual property that I call the piratical *ethos*. Such an analysis should reveal disjunctures and concordances among copyrightists, copyleftists, and pirates, revising assumptions concerning digital piracy while also highlighting the accuracy or misidentification of piratical motivation in both popular and academic discourse.

## METHODS

### Research Site and Demographics

Data were collected from six different BitTorrent communities.[1] Sometimes referred to as "file sharing communities" or "digital communes," private BitTorrent communities exhibit the characteristics of other file-sharing services only inasmuch as they provide links to downloadable content (Khambatti, Ryu, & Dasgupta, 2002). Fundamental differences between private BitTorrent communities in this study and publicly accessible BitTorrent websites such as The Pirate Bay or Demonoid include sustained user engagement over time, community-imposed quality control of archives, and coordinated group activity from various users—as opposed to just site administrators—to complete communal projects. In this sense, ties created within these communities of practice (Lave & Wenger, 1991) tend to be strong, yielding cohesive units that use latitudinal organization and consensus-building to make decisions concerning site development, rules and structure.[2] User intentionality in the sites is likewise strong, as members are committed to file-sharing aspects of the community: the cultivation of a clean, consistent archive, and enforcement of site rules by all users.

---

[1]I anonymized community names in this study to protect users from scrutiny or prosecution in countries where content industries have prosecuted or continue to prosecute BitTorrent site administrators. Hence, they will go under these acronyms: G###.net, P###.fm, P###.org, Q###.cd, T###.org and E###.org.

[2]For a more thorough description of private torrent sites, see Andersson Schwarz (2015).

Perhaps the most difficult aspect of providing demographic information about piratical sites of research is the inherent anonymity of members. Users employ pseudonyms to protect their identity from content industry observers who are also members of the community. Beyond counts of total site users, little information about the race, gender, or age of community members is available.

While users operate in relative anonymity, their subject positioning as members of communities of practice dedicated to participatory archival creation and curation contributes to their capacity to perform tropes that recur in such spaces. As members of private BitTorrent communities, individuals that provide the data for this study are familiar with the culture, ideals, attitudes, and motivations that feed such tropes; further, their participation in site forums is likely indicative of a path dependency wherein users consistently perform the tropes commonly associated with common discoursal arcs. To avoid an overemphasis on the demographic information of community members, I follow Andersson Schwarz and Larsson's (2013) work on piratical justification, concerning myself less with the biographic or ethnographic characteristics of site users, and instead focusing on the "specimens of reasoning" that characterize the piratical *ethos*.

Without server side permissions to access user IP addresses, it is impossible to provide substantive information about user distribution. This is especially unfortunate when considering the geographic spread of users in niche sites as this information might provide insights into the kinds of media appropriation carried out by users in developing economies. Luckily, members of Q###.cd provide some community demographics to all community members. Utilizing a combination of server side user statistics reports and GoogleCharts, a developer team at Q###.cd produced several interesting infographics on user distribution.

Based on the information available, Q###.cd users are overwhelmingly from North America (Figure 1). Further, citizens of developed economies constitute the vast majority of site users. Yet, users from developing and non-English speaking countries also frequent the site. Users from countries that are technologically advanced and have histories of relatively lax intellectual property application comprise the largest non-U.S. user base. Canadians, Swedes, Russians, Dutch, and Norwegians are represented in six of the top eight countries of origin.

These statistics suggest that Q###.cd is an inherently transnational space marked by English as *lingua franca*. This is not to suggest parity between site users from different nation states in the digital public sphere—undoubtedly the interests of US and Canadian users are the most

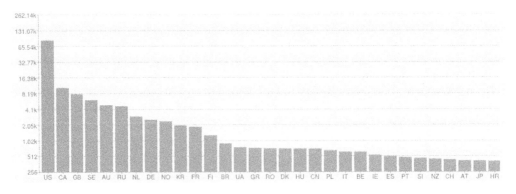

FIGURE 1  Q###.cd members' country of origin.

visible and vocal. Instead, what we should glean from Figure 1 is that sites are transnational activity systems, accessed by a wide-ranging group of users from most parts of the globe. Unbounded by geography and centered on an organized community of practice, communities like Q###.cd provide models of distributed collaboration that create strong ties among members from vastly different economic and political scenes. These relationships and collaborative acts factor prominently into the "specimens of reasoning" pirates use to justify their practice.

## Data Acquisition

Relying on Im and Chee (2006), this project assumes that asynchronous, threaded forum postings are valuable qualitative data because they provide observable, easy to access archives of user statements that cannot otherwise be gathered using face to face research methods. Especially in the case of geographically and temporally distributed research subjects, online forums hold credible, dependable, confirmable, and transferable records of individual perspectives from disparate socioeconomic and political contexts. The data were gathered in three separate harvests that occurred in four month intervals between May 2011 and May 2012. After identifying forum threads related to the topic of "intellectual property" in May 2011, each thread was revisited two additional times to collect any postings not included in the initial harvest. While the credibility and dependability of postings are a direct result of the technologies that structure participation in online forums, the confirmability and transferability of data are much more difficult to achieve as they rely on researcher interpretation. Below, I will discuss the four coding schema used in this study in detail, providing evidence of the credibility of each while also highlighting that their transferability is limited to other research sites that share particular contextual factors.

## Data Reduction

Selection of the full data set in this study utilized criterion-based sampling (Geisler, 2004). The corpus of appropriate data gathered in threads from site forums included the words "intellectual property," "copyright," and "piracy." This produced an initial corpus of 63 threaded conversations; 18 threads that intimately considered the philosophy, application, or ethics of intellectual property in digital environments were analyzed in detail.

After selecting the initial corpus, data were segmented to isolate observable units wherein the aforementioned reasoning occurred. Segmenting data by speaker produced individual units containing multiple divergent attitudes toward intellectual property. Hence, the smaller topical chain unit was employed. As a segment that allows participants to understand that conversation is *about* something, the topical chain provides t-unit clusters that coalesce around a particular idea or object in the world. In this way, complex ideas and situations are rendered observable and data is made segmentable into coherent, independent units. After segmenting the entire data set into 1,379 topical chains, I developed coding schema to categorize piratical reasoning toward intellectual property, copyright, and piracy.

## Coding Schema Development and Implementation

Coding schema provide the means to render data rhetorical, theoretical, and empirical (Smagorinsky, 2008). The process of developing coding schema in this research study progressed thus:

- sample selection and identification of marked contrasts;
- selective coding to identify different perspectives on intellectual property;
- creation of nested coding scheme for fine-grained analysis of divergent attitudes toward intellectual property resistance; and
- development of four coding schema to address polyvalent specimens of reasoning by research subjects.

In the process of initial sample selection I isolated 50 individual units that exhibited marked contrasts to one another, yielding a spectrum of opinions on intellectual property (Table 1).

The wide range of attitudes toward intellectual property in the initial sample transformed the initial methodology in important ways. First, data in "support" or "resistance" to intellectual property went deeper than a simple two-option count. The first tier coding process coded each segment for support/resistance/neither. This initial coding produced isolated segments that would be coded again based on reasoning in support of or in resistance to intellectual property. After coding the sample topical chains for support/resistance/neither, a disproportionately large number of segments were coded as "resistance." To discover the nuanced positions inside "resistance," additional coding schema were created, tested and revised.

To generate the particular categories for the resistance scheme, data were used to ground the analysis (Glaser & Strauss, 1967); furthermore, because researcher disassociation from previous

TABLE 1
Excerpt From Initial Sample Selection

| Speaker | Site | Thread | Segment |
|---|---|---|---|
| 3 | Q###.cd | Fed Up? | Piracy is basically theft. You can argue semantics, in that a download $=/=$ a lost sale, but you cannot argue that we're thieves. |
| 11 | Q###.cd | Fed Up? | I can pay for music or I can keep my money. Obviously, I'd rather just keep my money. It's simply a financial decision. |
| 34 | P###.fm | IP Necessary? | Science is co-operative. The idea that one person invents something all on their own isn't that valid very often. Even art I suppose could be argued is never original, it builds on influences from before and is created with other people. |
| 2 | T###.org | Why IP? | I tend, myself, to see overly constrictive IP law as a hindrance, a chokehold on real creativity. |
| 5 | E###.org | Knowledge Free? | Copyright is evil because I cannot think of any other option than Knowledge must be free - it is necessary for the good of our fellow man. |
| 7 | P###.fm | IP Necessary? | Major built-out electronic medical record systems, for example, cost hundreds of thousands of dollars to develop and scale - why shouldn't companies that innovate things like that be legally allowed to protect them? |

TABLE 2
Comparison of Categories of Resistance Between Scheme 1 and Scheme 4

| Scheme 1 Categories: Resistance | Definition | Scheme 4 Categories: Resistance | Definition |
|---|---|---|---|
| Creative Hindrance | Code as *creative hindrance* (CH) any t-unit that references the human production as constrained/hindered by intellectual property. | Public Good | Code as *public good* (P) any topical chain that resists IP on the grounds that it damages the public interest. |
| Imbalance | Code as *imbalance* (I) any t-unit that claims that the current copyright regime is out of balance in favor of content owners, not authors/creators or the public interest. | Economic | Code as *economic* (E) any topical chain that references financials as the justification for resistance to IP. |
| Anti-Capitalist | Code as *anti-capitalist* (AC) any t-unit that contains a reference to how IP supports economic interests instead of altruistic human motives or claims information and knowledge shouldn't be property. | Apathy | Code as *apathy* (A) any topical chain that references theft or "just because" as justification for resistance to IP. |
| Technological Change | Code as *technological change* (TC) any t-unit that contains a reference to how changes in technology have transformed intellectual property. | Technological | Code as *technological* (T) any topical chain that references technologies as the justification for resistance to IP. |
| Other | Code as *other* (O) any t-unit that does not contain any of the aforementioned codes. | Other | Code as *other* (O) any topical chain that does not contain any of the aforementioned codes. |

readings on intellectual property was impossible, a process of induction followed whereby the researcher coordinated instances when the data echoed arguments traced in previous research, and vice-versa. Unfortunately, results of the initial coding revealed too much emphasis on categories derived from previous knowledge and not enough attention to the data.[3] When calculated for inter rater reliability, the initial resistance scheme achieved only 64% agreement. After reviewing where coders disagreed, I found that many segments claimed apathy as a reason to resist intellectual property. After multiple revisions that pushed the coding scheme further and further away from researcher perspective and closer to the data itself, exclusive yet flexible categories able to accommodate the range of resistances that appeared in the data were used to structure the coding schema (Table 2).

[3] Andersson Schwarz and Larsson (2013) recognize the tendency to frame data in familiar tropes in their review of a selection of 75,000 piratical perspectives on file-sharing. Noting that "As researchers, we tend to overestimate those tropes that are of great significance to us" because of their frequency and familiarity in academic literature, the authors highlight how particular tropes and modes of reasoning are grounded in specific locales. Paying close attention to those spaces allows for grounded analyses that push against the common tropes that circulate as "specimens of reasoning" in academic circles or in industry-sponsored discourse.

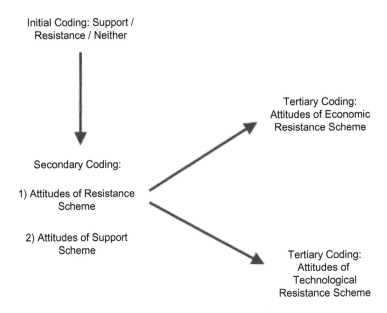

FIGURE 2  Nested coding plan.

After developing a measurable, reliable coding scheme for the varieties of resistance to intellectual property, I returned to the overall coding plan, looking for additional attitudes embedded in the discourse. Eventually, a nested coding plan was developed. It coded for the attitudes toward intellectual property, piracy, and copyright that appeared most frequently in the data (Figure 2).

The nested coding plan resulted in four coding schema: 1) Attitudes of Resistance Scheme, 2) Attitudes of Support Scheme, 3) Attitudes of Economic Resistance Scheme, and 4) Attitudes of Technological Resistance Scheme (Table 3). After achieving a concordance rate of 88% for simple interrater reliability with the initial sample across the nested coding scheme, the entire data set was coded.

TABLE 3
Coding Schema

| Attitudes of Support<br>*Secondary Coding* | Attitudes of Resistance<br>*Secondary Coding* | Attitudes of Economic<br>Resistance<br>*Tertiary Coding* | Attitudes of Technological<br>Resistance<br>*Tertiary Coding* |
|---|---|---|---|
| Sweat of the Brow | Public | Anti-Corporate | Convenience |
| Theft | Economic | Preview | Definition |
| Artist Rights | Technological | Direct Contribution | Social |
| Protection | Apathy | Funds | Quality |

# FINDINGS

The three-tiered coding method revealed complex and often contradictory piratical reasoning toward intellectual property, copyright and piracy (Table 4). While resistance toward intellectual property comprised the majority of codable segments (82%), attitudes of support also play an integral role in understanding piratical reasoning. Further, economic and technological attitudes of resistance warranted further inspection as they comprised a majority of codable resistance segments (69%). In the following sections, the findings of this analysis are correlated with prominent themes from academic and popular discourse; in particular, the technological-social and economic anti-corporate resistances are highlighted as they comprise the largest portions of the overall dataset (Figure 3).

TABLE 4
Complete Findings of Analysis

| Coding Level | Coding Schema Categories | Totals | Percentages |
|---|---|---|---|
| **Level 1** | R/S/N - Resistance Total Count | 1134 | 82.23% |
| | R/S/N - Support Total Count | 146 | 10.58% |
| | R/S/N - Neither Resistance or Support | 99 | 7.18% |
| | | 1379 | |
| **Level 2** | Resistance - Public Total Count | 157 | 13.84% |
| | Resistance - Economic Total Count | 421 | 37.13% |
| | Resistance - Technological Total Count | 372 | 32.80% |
| | Resistance - Apathy Total Count | 87 | 7.67% |
| | Resistance - Other Total Count | 97 | 8.56% |
| | | 1134 | |
| | Support - Sweat of the Brow Total Count | 49 | 33.56% |
| | Support - Theft Total Count | 27 | 18.49% |
| | Support - Artist Rights Total Count | 13 | 8.90% |
| | Support - Protection Total Count | 39 | 26.71% |
| | Support - Other Total Count | 17 | 12.33% |
| | | 146 | |
| **Level 3** | Economic - Anti-Corporate Total Count | 175 | 41.57% |
| | Economic - Preview Total Count | 67 | 15.91% |
| | Economic - Direct Contribution Total Count | 70 | 16.63% |
| | Economic - Funds Total Count | 94 | 22.33% |
| | Economic - Other Total Count | 15 | 3.56% |
| | | 421 | |
| | Technological - Convenience Total Count | 122 | 32.80% |
| | Technological - Definition Total Count | 61 | 16.40% |
| | Technological - Social Total Count | 146 | 38.83% |
| | Technological - Quality Total Count | 33 | 8.87% |
| | Technological - Other Total Count | 10 | 2.69% |
| | | 372 | |

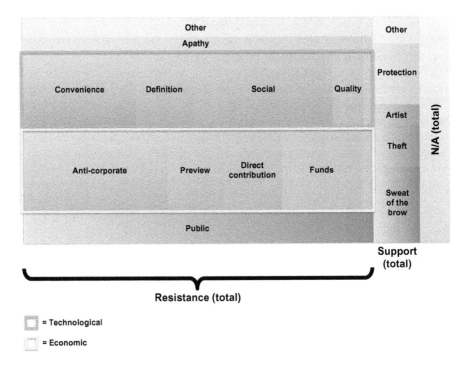

FIGURE 3  Visualization of study findings.

## Technological Resistance

Despite comprising the second largest contingent of data, attitudes of technological resistance, reveal the most salient aspects of the piratical *ethos*. Notably, user responses in this section emphasize the intersection of technology, community, and sociality in sustaining BitTorrent communities. Focusing on sharing technologies as instruments of exposure and discovery, technological attitudes highlight the anachronistic application of analog intellectual property paradigms in the face of deep integration between technology and community in digital spaces. Segments coded as technological also draw attention to file sharing as an intensely social act that generates wealth and provides alternative avenues of exposure for creators. Some technological defenses explicitly relate to digital rights management technologies and standards of media quality; these positions suggest that consumers wish to control when, where, and how they consume content. More commonly, though, segments coded as "technological" draw attention to the role of community and the social in the construction of the piratical *ethos*.

Writing before the explosion of Facebook in the late 2000s, Benkler (2006) notes that arguments concerning the function, influence, and effects of digital social relations tend toward the hyperbolic. While social participation enabled by the Internet does influence individual experience, it does not result in the complete breakdown of face-to-face society, and neither does it create transcendent virtual communities. Benkler suggests instead that the effects of virtual social networks are twofold: first, a "thickening" of social relations with preexisting friends, neighbors, and family is facilitated through social networking; second, and more importantly, virtual community creates what Benkler calls "limited-purpose, loose relationships," or virtual links between individuals engaged in group-based collaboration with shared purposes toward shared goals. In the years since Benkler's study, social networks have exploded in accessibility, usability and popularity, highlighting the complex intertwining that occurs among individual users, communities of practice, and technologies that facilitate social exchange. All of these components result in the production of social relations that redirect agency and attitude, forming alternative subjectivities that provide new modes of digital connection. Comprising the largest amount of technology resistance segments (39%), data coded "social" are more important than their 10.60% of the entire dataset conveys. Inherently, invite-only BitTorrent sites are communities and the activities that occur therein must be understood as community-driven. Because "community" plays a part in constructing the piratical *ethos*, all of the categories reviewed in the "technological resistance" schema have a social element.

The difference between piratical BitTorrent communities and other file-sharing technologies like cyberlockers ("one-click hosting" sites), direct peer-to-peer transfers, and Usenet newsgroup binaries, is the community-oriented nature of these sites. Obviously, this analysis investigates forum postings—themselves social spaces wherein users dialogue on a variety of different topics. Beyond forums, sites like T###.org and Q###.cd facilitate social exchange through a range of technological tools and mediating technologies that deserve their own analysis in another work; however, it is clear that the "social" aspects of piratical practice are important to understanding piratical motivation. Many segments coded as social make reference to piracy as a form of social media—an alternative press that creates interest around bands that are not a part of the Big Media ecosystem (Bohn, 2012; Love, 2000). These segments also spotlight the sociality and technological mediation of digital circulation, revealing how taste gains rhetorical velocity and metastasizes across digital media ecologies (Fuller, 2007). Other segments explicitly reference the influence of the community itself, revealing how site participation motivates piratical acts as much as media acquisition. Still other segments highlight the role of social technologies that create moments of discovery wherein users move through metadata networks to find new media:

> More listeners - more music. Period.
>     - Lin,[4] P###.fm
>     A truly talented artists [sic] no longer needs the push of a major label in order to sell records - if their music is good enough, the word of mouth of millions of people on the Internet will do it for them.
>     - Kamaji, Q###.cd

Many of the segments coded "social" in the technological resistance scheme justified piracy on the grounds that any monetary loss by the artist or author would be compensated through exposure over social media. Users adopting this attitude offered a two-fold defense that first presented a definitional argument about the difference between copying and theft. After justifying their practice as sharing, not stealing, the users then argued that sharing results in greater exposure and potentially more sales for the creator. In these two segments, Boh in the Q###.cd thread "Music Piracy" argues:

---

[4] All user handles have been changed to protect the anonymity of site users in this study.

> First, copying isn't stealing. I'm not depriving anyone of a physical thing. It might be morally debatable, but it's not theft. And besides by sharing music we're helping people get into bands they wouldn't have the opportunity to get into otherwise which means more t-shirts, stickers, concert tickets and CDs get sold that wouldn't have been sold otherwise.

Segments following this two-step defense draw attention to circulation and velocity in networked information ecologies. Users such as Boh recognize the nonrivalrous nature of digital media, defending their piratical practice by shifting infringement from economic to moral frames.[5] Boh also foregrounds the importance of circulation and velocity for digital commodities, noting that without exposure, there is little opportunity for sales. Implicitly, Boh is arguing that because electronic media are nonrivalrous, circulation and velocity are impeded by intellectual property control mechanisms. Circumventing the sanctioned systems of distribution to generate interest by other community members and the networks they are attached to outside piratical spaces is actually a beneficent action that helps artists thrive commercially. Case studies of artists who employ piratical BitTorrent communities to drive interest and sales appear to bear out this claim (Hammond, 2013).

While the majority of segments coded "social" make the increased visibility argument, others emphasize site membership and community participation as the key motivator for sharing. P###.fm user Yuna states simply, "It's all about the community, eh?" In an elaborated post, Yubaba in the thread "How Do You Justify Piracy?" argues that:

> Imagine whole community of people with people who have immense expertise in every genres (except for Jungle)—that's what we have here. And if I even have a fleeting interest in a genre I haven't heard, all I have to do is head to these forums and start a thread asking *for* an introduction to it or post in an existing one, the people here are happy to give help as long as you're going to listen to it. I can't just walk into a record store and hope the clerk knows something about Norweigen [sic] roots Black Metal or Early twenties blues, they may well be an expert but it's awfully optimistic. Our community is the future of music sharing and music is a communal experience, right?

Highlighting the community's role in exposing what Anderson (2006) calls long-tail, niche media, Yubaba exhibits a common attitude in piratical communities: organization and site activity is facilitated by social acts of sharing and communication. Without these elements, it is unlikely many individuals would participate with such commitment over time.

Last but not least, a sizeable portion of the "social" segments make direct reference to the role of sharing technologies. Most activities in piratical communities are mediated by technological interfaces: browser plugins provide network graphs of related genres and artists, specialized code allows users to curate personal collections, and core tracker functionalities provide users information on the most popular downloads. These technologies make the downloading experience a social event, enabled by the time and effort invested by site users to upload, share, tag, and download content. Haku on the Q###.cd thread "The Ethics of Piracy" exhibits such an attitude, noting that "the other benefit is the discovery of new band/artists through other users and the

---

[5] In Andersson Schwarz's analysis of Swedish file-sharers (2012), he discovers much the same shift away from economic frameworks toward civic or moral lenses. Noting that many file-sharers justify their practice in "civic" modes that highlight cultural access to digital content as a fundamental human right, Andersson Schwarz (2012) draws attention to the rhetorical redirection pirates use to downplay economic/industrial indictments of intellectual property infringement.

linking functions of plugins like Oink+."[6] Users such as Haku highlight the role that mediating technologies play in making piracy a social experience and draw attention to the reciprocal agency distributed across human users and digital tools in piratical spaces.

Other technological resistances included statements rooted in definition, quality, and convenience. Of the three, users claiming a convenience argument underscore the incapacities of media distribution systems like iTunes and Amazon to meet user demand for niche media.[7] Congruently, users claiming a quality resistance reject digital big media on an anti-DRM basis, arguing that consumer control trumps the convenience of purchasing digital media from corporate distributors. In arguments that reflect popular discourses concerning the need for a digital copyright regime (Boyle, 2010; Cohen, 2012), these pirates point out the problematic use of property metaphors for describing ubiquitous and infinitely reproducible digital media.

## Economic Resistance

Unsurprisingly, pirates are not keen on corporations; in fact, there is something to the notion that pirates consider themselves digital Robin Hoods, pilfering from the excesses of Big Media and redistributing cultural wealth to the people. Anti-corporate sentiment toward Big Media is common among pirates and can be understood as a strong reaction to the file sharer prosecution. Individuals in the anti-corporate camp hope to deal economic damage to the content industry, arguing that continued prosecution of file-sharers by the Recording Industry Association of America (RIAA), Motion Picture Association of America (MPAA), and others is an outdated and terroristic business model. Suggesting that piracy could be a boon to the content industries, these users question why Big Media continues to persecute its own customers.

Without a doubt, the most prominent attitude coded in this entire analysis indicted the RIAA and MPAA in anti-corporate justifications for infringement. User Chihiro on P###.fm argued, "I disapprove of the RIAA and its tactics. I made a pledge to never buy a CD from RIAA labels. I either pirate it or buy it used so that they won't get my money." Chihiro justifies resisting intellectual property by invoking the corporate greed of these organizations:

> At this point every action I've seen taken to protect media rights appears as a poorly veiled refusal to lose a single precious cent. Even if that cent is earned at the cost of suing, harassing, and really hurting people I believe are innocent. The media moguls have become entirely too greedy and willing to take advantage of both their consumers and artists.

As many scholars observe, content industry campaigns to combat piracy utilize rhetorics of fear and intimidation instead of engaging users on the ethics of file sharing (Lessig, 2005; Logie, 2006; Reyman, 2010). Patry (2009) underscores this claim, demonstrating how "moral panics" are perpetuated by content industry watchdogs to whip up public opinion against piracy in the service of Big Media-friendly legislation. Recognizing that the ultimate goal of anti-piracy campaigns is to move citizens from "criminal" to "consumer," the media and discourse of organizations such

---

[6]Oink+ is a browser plugin that links different uploads via user-generated tagging systems and metadata housed at social music sites like Last.fm.

[7]With the increasing adoption of streaming media services such as Amazon Prime, Netflix, and Spotify, one wonders how long the "Convenience" justification will hold weight.

as the RIAA employ what Andersson Schwarz (2012) characterizes as an "industrial" frame for understanding file-sharing. This form of reasoning assumes *a priori* that file sharers are criminals because they subvert the capitalist economic order. Ignoring the multiple motivations revealed in this analysis generates remarkable ire among file sharers, creating a rhetorical moment wherein pirates and Big Media are suspicious of each other's motives. Both sides end up levying charges of moral corruption; further, the sentiment expressed in segments of anti-corporate economic resistance become concretized attitudes that continue to structure file sharer perception of the content industry. San, in the thread "How do you justify piracy?" adopts this exact attitude toward anti-file sharing campaigns, noting that piracy becomes a form of civil disobedience against hegemonic corporate and media interests. She claims:

> I justify it [piracy] by reading the news and seeing the media mirroring bs the RIAA/MPAA/etc. say and regard it as truth. I see myself pirating as an act against this kind of fallacy/lies/deceit that the corporations try to put forward to the typical citizen.

The anti-corporate form of resistance reveals important details about piratical reasoning. First, anti-piracy rhetoric almost never has the intended effect; rather, it often consolidates and solidifies latent anti-corporate sentiments and provides consumers an easy, relatively anonymous means of circumventing industry control over distribution and circulation (Committee on Intellectual Property Rights in the Emerging Information Infrastructure and the National Research Council, 2000). Second, because resisting corporate control through acts of file sharing becomes an anti-hegemonic, liberatory act, many individuals contesting intellectual property on these grounds become invested in their piratical acts because they carry political implications. This investment sustains piratical participation and actually grows the file-sharing movement. Major studios and other content industry players would do wise to heed the advice of Q###.cd user Gonza: "The more the RIAA keeps pushing against file sharing, the more I'll download." To reclaim a sizeable portion of their market and redeem industry image, record labels, movie studios, and book publishers will need to work against anti-corporate attitudes by addressing the concerns raised in this section.

Other resistances to intellectual property and copyright on economic bases included segments coded as "Preview," "Direct contribution," and "Funds." Preview resistances made reference to the high-cost, low-reward practice of purchasing an entire album or book on digital download without a preview. Arguments from this perspective relied on disappointing analog experiences in media consumption. Direct contributionists often took an implicitly anti-corporate tack, arguing that they would rather directly contribute money to artists by attending shows and buying merchandise than see publishers and distribution companies capitalize on the labors of others. Finally, economic resistances coded as "Funds" drew attention to the overpricing of digital media—especially in light of diminishing quality of albums in an age of single song downloads.

## Support

Reasoning in support of intellectual property supports Andersson Schwarz and Larsson's (2013) findings that pirates sometimes exhibit "market optimism" toward the industrial and commercial orders that structure media production and distribution. Coding in this study suggests that some pirates justify intellectual property based on liberal humanist theories of the subject whose roots lie in Locke and the Romantics; furthermore, other attitudes of support draw heavily upon ideals of protection and incentive for creators. Defenders of intellectual property are also quick to point out the differences between patents, trademarks, and copyrights. These defenses often support protections for patents and trademarks while remaining ambivalent or skeptical about copyright.

Comprising the largest percentage of support, segments coded as "Sweat of the brow" argue that creators are entitled to the fruits of their labor. Relying on Locke's theory of "labor-mixing," supporters couch their arguments in economic terms, noting that while changes in technology have precipitated new modes of distribution, these transformations are not justifications for ignoring intellectual property. In the P###.fm thread "How do you justify piracy?" Eboshi notes that "Artists need and deserve our remuneration . . . . Shows and merch are not enough . . . especially for authors. How do they come to your town or print on a t-shirt if they don't have any money?" Recognizing that direct contribution to artists is basically impossible if they fail to have the capital to tour and secure merchandise, Eboshi draws attention to the "vicious circle" of piracy: without initial purchases of media in physical or digital forms, most artists cannot fund publicity for tours or produce items to sell to the consumer directly. Because of this circle, the reasoning goes, emerging artists and other creatives need intellectual property protections to capitalize on their works.

Considering the question, "Is intellectual property necessary?" Toki on Q###.cd provides a complex answer that relies on the "sweat of the brow" defense while at the same time criticizing the entire system of intellectual property. She observes:

> I'm thoroughly "anticapitalist" in most regards, but considering the entire system is catered to the faceless supply-side of creators, i.e. rightholders, it stands to reason that when the opportunity for Joe Schmoe to benefit from his creation as opposed to someone else, he should have the legal means to ensure his place among the other capitalists, who would want nothing more than to profit off the backs of others doing the work.

Toki highlights a prominent pattern observed throughout claims of support; namely, she understands and justifies intellectual property protections pragmatically, considering the way that the current system is organized; however, philosophically, she opposes an entire system wherein art and culture are rendered commodities.

Users who claimed a protection support for intellectual property consistently demonstrated a deeper, more nuanced understanding of the judicial and legislative foundations of intellectual property and copyright. This is evidenced by the strict attention to the differences between the three domains of intellectual property: patents, trademarks, and copyrights. Exhibiting "industrial" modes of reasoning, responders in this category relied on the spirit of protection in the US Constitutional Copyright Clause, tethering research, development, and advance in technology and science to incentives created by a "monopoly for limited time" of the intellectual property holder. Other supporters noted that piracy is theft. Finally, those arguing for artists' rights constituted the smallest percentage of support, suggesting that American notions of copyright that downplay the creator of copyrighted works but elevate the owner of the copyrights may more strongly structure reasoning of support.

## CONCLUSION

The preceding analysis presents a modest attempt at tracing the "subject" of piratical spaces by paying special attention to discussions regarding intellectual property, copyright, and piracy. Following the "social turn" in the Humanities, this chapter recognizes that an individual's subjectivity is a socialized product of cultural and historical development, constructed from outside through the myriad connectivities that constitute experience inside community. Outside influence is deeply embedded in an individual's attitudes, ideologies and modes of reasoning, allowing the attitudinal arrangement of cords and knots that compete within our psyches to *appear* whole and given. Unwinding these competing attitudes from the knot of the self, this article attempted to answer the question, "Who are the subjects of piratical activity?" with the answer, "Attitudes X, Y, and Z are the most important and prevalent specimens of reasoning that construct piratical identity in private BitTorrent communities."

Though they comprise a small percentage of the overall dataset, specimens of reasoning in support of intellectual property are a fascinating window into the economic, or in Andersson Schwarz's language, "industrial" frames for supporting intellectual property. Though this analysis did not confirm Andersson Schwarz's (2012) findings that many file sharers inevitably see piracy integrated with market-based distribution of media, justifications for support in this study do confirm the notion that a portion of pirates understand and appreciate the core values of capitalist production; namely, the importance of monetary compensation for creative production and the import of the profit motive.

By count, data conveying technological tropes prove less abundant than economic tropes; however, technological resistances convey a fascinating synergy among communication sharing technologies and the communities who organize their activities around them. Users adopting "social" technological opposition to intellectual property foreground the essential role that networks and mediating technologies play in artist discovery, exposure, and community development. Despite not using analytic terms, the modes of argumentation exhibiting social tropes recognize the potential of heightened digital circulation and increased rhetorical velocity, frequently referring to the role that social technologies and social media play in the sharing of media. Other technological tropes hinged on the non-rivalrous nature of digital artifacts, the inadequacy of formalized distribution networks, and the inferior quality provided under current media consumption outlets. The prevalence of the technological, in both social and medial milieux, suggests new research into piracy might take into account the complex relationship among social connection, tool design, and user activity to produce more accurate renderings of where we are and where we are going with respect to intellectual property and digital artifacts in community spaces like invite-only BitTorrent trackers.

Attitudes of economic resistance characterize the majority of segments coded in this study and overwhelmingly convey a deep distrust of corporate control in the content industries. Advocating a return to localized media and a circumvention of the intermediary role entertainment conglomerates play in the production process, users addressing economic tropes look to alternative models such as crowdfunding and direct contribution to reward creatives for their labor. Attitudes of economic resistance to intellectual property also highlight unreasonably high pricing systems and the inability to "try-before-you-buy" when making media purchases. If media companies, both big and small, hope to recuperate their image and meet future consumer demand, they may consider listening to the attitudes of economic resistance revealed in this study rather than continuing campaigns that pirates perceive as fear-mongering and even terroristic.

Attitudes of resistance also disclose a small but vocal portion of users who argue against intellectual property because of its constriction of the public domain. Relying on a host of utilitarian, cultural-ecological, "sweat of the brow," and Romantic arguments, these users most closely align with academic and legal contestations of copyright, providing arguments for and against the expansion or control of copyright. Considering the relatively small number of appearances of these attitudes in this analysis, academics and legal scholars approaching the piracy problem pragmatically might look outside long-standing theoretical articulations of intellectual property in favor of listening to the pirates themselves. This grounded approach may well lead to more parity between experts and practitioners, eschewing the academic missionary model (Andersson Schwarz & Larsson, 2013; Segal, Pare, Brent, & Vipond, 1998) that dominates the discourse at present, allowing the discourse of piratical resistance to better incorporate the viewpoints of all those invested in the problems and promise of intellectual property in the digital age.

## REFERENCES

Anderson, C. (2006). *The long tail: Why the future of business is selling less of more*. New York, NY: Hyperion.

Andersson Schwarz, J. (2012). Learning from the file-sharers: Civic modes of justification versus industrial ones. *Arts Marketing: An International Journal, 2*(2), 104–117.

Andersson Schwarz, J. (2015). Catering for whom? The problematic ethos of audiovisual distribution online. In V. Crisp & G. Menotti Gonring (Eds.), *Besides the screen: Moving images through distribution, promotion and curation*. London, England: Palgrave Macmillan.

Andersson Schwarz, J., & Larsson, S. (2013). The justifications of piracy: Differences in conceptualization and argumentation between active uploaders and other file-sharers. In M. Fredriksson & J. Arvanitakis (Eds.), *Piracy: Leakages from modernity*. Los Angeles, CA: Litwin Books.

Barlow, J. P. (1994, September). The economy of ideas. *Wired, 2*.

Benkler, Y. (2006). *The wealth of networks: How social production transforms markets and freedom*: New Haven, CT: Yale University Press.

Biagioli, M. (2011). Genius against copyright: Revisiting Fichte's proof of the illegality of reprinting. *Notre Dame Law Review, 86*(5), 1847–1868.

Bohn, D. (2012). Neil Young on music and Steve Jobs: 'Piracy is the new radio.' *The Verge*. Retrieved from http://www.theverge.com/2012/1/31/2761597/neil-young-music-steve-jobs-piracy-is-the-new-radio

Boyle, J. (1997). A politics of intellectual property: Environmentalism for the net. *Duke Law Journal, 47*(1), 87–116.

Boyle, J. (2003). The second enclosure movement and the construction of the public domain. *Law and Contemporary Problems, 66*, 33–74.

Boyle, J. (2010). *The public domain: Enclosing the commons of the mind*. New Haven, CT: Yale University Press.

Cohen, J. E. (2012). *Configuring the networked self: Law, code, and the play of everyday practice*. New Haven, CT: Yale University Press.

Committee on Intellectual Property Rights in the Emerging Information Infrastructure & National Research Council. (2000). *The digital dilemma: Intellectual property in the information age*. Washington, DC: National Academy Press.

Cummings, A. (2013). *Democracy of sound: Music piracy and the remaking of American copyright in the twentieth century*. New York, NY: Oxford University Press.

DeVoss, D. N., & Porter, J. E. (2006). Why Napster matters to writing: Filesharing as a new ethic of digital delivery. *Computers and Composition, 23*(2), 178–210.

Doctorow, C. (2008). *Content: Selected essays on technology, creativity, copyright, and the future of the future*. San Francisco, CA: Tachyon.

Fuller, M. (2007). *Media ecologies: Materialist energies in art and technoculture*. Cambridge, MA: MIT Press.

Geisler, C. (2004). *Analyzing streams of language: Twelve steps to the systematic coding of text, talk, and other verbal data*. New York, NY: Pearson.

Glaser, B. G., & Strauss, A. (1967). *The discovery of grounded theory; strategies for qualitative research*. Chicago, IL: Aldine.

Halbert, D. J. (2005). *Resisting intellectual property law*. New York, NY: Routledge.

Hammond, R. G. (2013). Profit leak? Pre-release file sharing and the music industry. *Southern Economic Journal*, *81*(2), 387–408.

Hawk, B. (2012). Curating ecologies, circulating musics. In S. Dobrin (Ed.), *Ecology, writing theory, and new media* (pp. 160–179). New York, NY: Routledge.

Im, E., & Chee, W. (2006). An online forum as a qualitative research method: Practical issues. *Nursing Research*, *55*(4), 267–273.

Johns, A. (2011). *Piracy: The intellectual property wars from Gutenberg to Gates*. Chicago, IL: University of Chicago Press.

Kennedy, K., & Howard, R. M. (2013). Introduction to the special issue on western cultures of intellectual property. *College English*, *75*(5), 461–469.

Khambatti, M., Ryu, K. D., & Dasgupta, P. (2002). *Peer-to-peer communities: Formation and discovery*. Paper presented at the IASTED PDCS, Cambridge, MA.

Lave, J., & Wenger, E. (1991). *Situated learning: Legitimate peripheral participation*. Cambridge, England: Cambridge University Press.

Lessig, L. (2005). *Free culture: The nature and future of creativity*. New York, NY: Penguin.

Lessig, L. (2008). *Remix: Making art and commerce thrive in the hybrid economy*. New York, NY: Penguin.

Lindgren, S. (2012). The subpolitics of online piracy: A Swedish case study. *Convergence*, *18*(2), 143–164.

Lindgren, S. (2013). Pirate panics: Comparing news and blog discourse on illegal filesharing in Sweden. *Information, Communication and Society*, 1–24.

Locke, J. (1980). *Second treatise of government*. Indianapolis, IN: Hackett.

Logie, J. (2006). *Peers, pirates, and persuasion: Rhetoric in the peer-to-peer debates*. Anderson, SC: Parlor Press.

Love, C. (2000). Courtney Love does the math. *Salon*. Retrieved from http://www.salon.com/2000/06/14/love_7/

Mason, M. (2009). *The pirate's dilemma: How youth culture is reinventing capitalism*. New York, NY: Free Press.

Patry, W. (2009). *Moral panics and the copyright wars*. Oxford, England: Oxford University Press.

Reyman, J. (2010). *The rhetoric of intellectual property: Copyright law and the regulation of digital culture*. New York, NY: Routledge.

Rose, M. (1993). *Authors and owners: The invention of copyright*. Cambridge, MA: Harvard University Press.

Segal, J., Pare, A., Brent, D., & Vipond, D. (1998). The researcher as missionary: Problems with rhetoric and reform in the disciplines. *College Composition and Communication*, *50*(1), 71–90.

Smagorinsky, P. (2008). The methods section as conceptual epicenter in constructing social science research reports. *Written Communication*, *25*(3), 389–411.

Strangelove, M. (2005). *The empire of mind: Digital piracy and the anti-capitalist movement*. Toronto, Canada: University of Toronto Press.

Vaidhyanathan, S. (2001). *Copyrights and copywrongs: The rise of intellectual property and how it threatens creativity*. New York, NY: New York University Press.

Woodmansee, M. (1994). *The author, art, and the market: Rereading the history of aesthetics*. New York, NY: Columbia University Press.

Young, E. (1966). *Conjectures on original composition*. Leeds, England: Scholar Press.

# The Media Archaeology of File Sharing: Broadcasting Computer Code to Swedish Homes

Jörgen Skågeby

*Stockholm University*

What form did file sharing take before the internet's usage became mainstream, and what practices from that period remain? This article examines a Swedish radio show that broadcast listener-contributed computer code in the mid 1980s. It applies a combined theoretical framework of intermediality and sharing theory and argues that this combination is central to the analysis of piracy and social change. The results indicate an interesting paradox in terms of pushing and pulling content as the practice relied on both in public broadcasting as well as with contributing media users. As such, the case of *Datorernas värld* prefigures how peer interaction and sharing relies on more centralized and controlled channels of communication. The article historically situates themes such as intermediality, surveillance, gender representation, and piracy and provides a piece of computing history that is topical but, strangely, critically ignored.

## INTRODUCTION

In what form did file sharing exist before the internet moved from the military to the mainstream, and how have the practices formed then altered over time? The media archaeology of file sharing includes many enlightening experiments and media forms that prove informative when mapping out the logic of sharing that dominates today. Media archaeology can be described as "a heterogeneous set of theories and methods that investigate media history through its alternative roots, its forgotten paths, and neglected ideas and machines that still are useful when reflecting the supposed newness of digital culture" (Parikka, 2010, para. 2). As such, an important precondition for media-archaeological studies is to try to avoid reinforcing the present's supremacy. Rather than treating computing history as a linear trajectory, where the new always "kills" or replaces the old, media archaeology highlights the specific capacities of machinery which are then mapped out in relation to other specifics creating a cartographic, rather than teleological, account of media history. This article will take a closer look at one particular historical practice that combined public service broadcasting, the existing range of consumer media, and sharing logic. The analysis will focus specifically on a Swedish national radio show which was broadcast during the mid 1980s domestication of the home computer. The show consisted of two parts: one editorial, including reports, reviews, instructions, and speculations on the computer in society and in the home; and

77

the other consisted of actual computer code in audio format. The broadcasting of computer code-as-sound was made possible by the fact that many home computers used common cassette tapes as storage media. Home computer owners could record the broadcast code via their receivers and tape decks and then "load" the recordings into their computers via connected tape stations (Skågeby, 2008). While the computer programs that were broadcast were written by listeners themselves and therefore not pirated, this article will argue that piracy, in a wide sense, is bolstered by intermedial innovations and a popularization of the logic of sharing, aspects to which this radio show definitely contributed. Certainly, the case of radio broadcast computer code is but one of many examples of how current debates on file sharing can be historicized in the terms of media archaeology. This article will argue that, as one part of the nascent cartography of file sharing, it is a particularly fascinating phenomenon in the history of computing. The analysis will historically situate themes such as intermediality, surveillance, gender representation, and piracy and provide a piece of computing history, which is topical yet strangely underresearched.

## BACKGROUND AND MATERIAL: THE RADIO, HOME COMPUTERS, AND AUDIOCASSETTES

Between January 1985 and June 1986, the Swedish national radio broadcast the show *Datorernas värld*. The show is intriguing as it represents an early attempt at public, large-scale, wireless file sharing. The show transmitted computer code represented as sound, which could then be recorded onto audiocassettes by listeners all around Sweden. The cassette was a common storage medium used with home computers. Recorded programs could consequently be loaded into computers via tape stations. However, the heyday of the cassette in home computer culture was brief, and the show only lasted two years. Viewed as an experiment in popular wireless file sharing, many interesting and fascinating aspects come to the surface. For example, the storing of computer code on cassettes makes the cassette, for the first time, multimedial. When digital computer code could be represented as analogue sound and then converted back to digital code, it meant that recordings could be executed not only as sound and music, but as animations, graphics and "interaction logic." Further, *Datorernas värld* illustrates how sound, in the mid 1980s, was, although marginal, an in-use modality for computer communication. Interestingly, more recent stories have shown how sound is again used as a mode of communication in computer networks. Marks (2013) tells of a case where ultrasound signals can spread computer viruses. Also, Hanspach and Goetz describe how a "covert acoustical mesh network can be conceived as a botnet or malnet that is accessible via near-field audio communications" (2013, p. 758). This illustrates how the mapping out of previous media practices may reveal conceptual continuations and disruptions in the processes of media development and popular communication. It is interesting to see how code-as-sound is again regarded as a sociotechnical potential.

*Datorernas värld* was divided into two types of shows. One with editorial content, broadcast during the day, and one supplementary show with code transmissions, broadcast during night hours. The reason for the nighttime broadcasts was that when transmitted over the air, these computer programs sounded like some kind of metallic buzzing and gnarling (Lasar, 2012). The editorial content included reports from conferences, interviews with experts, surveys of foreign computer magazines, or walkthroughs, where a member of staff performed a specific task while concurrently describing the procedure. As an initial proof-of-concept, three two-part shows were broadcast to collect listener ideas and experiences. Opinions and feelings could be submitted via post or by calling the show's answering machine. Some of the listeners' calls were played during the show. Most of them were concerned with problems that occurred when recording code onto tape or when loading the programs into the computer. The hosts were, however, pragmatic and concluded that a "surprising" number of listeners had been successful in recording and executing the code. The show was given a go-ahead. Another fourteen two-part programs were broadcast over the following two years.

The theme tune for *Datorernas värld* was the track "It's more fun to compute" by German band Kraftwerk. Several of the tracks from their album *Computerwelt* (1981) are also used throughout the show, such as "Pocket Calculator." It was the only music included in the show. The choice of using Kraftwerk, and specifically *Computerwelt*, speaks to the tension between possibilities and fears that is expressed in the editorial content of the show. The album depicted a then-futuristic world of online dating and productive socio-technical interplay, but also of surveillance and control. A broad observation of the themes discussed in *Datorernas värld* presents the same general tension.

During 1985 and 1986, *Datorernas värld* broadcast about 90 programs sent in by listeners on cassette, split nearly evenly between games and "utility" programs. Recurring types of programs were random lotto number generators, foreign word tests, math tests, indexing programs, and simple games such as steering a spaceship onto a landing platform. A program took between ten seconds and nine minutes to broadcast. At the time, the market for home computers included a range of brands with different processors/operating systems, yet all used the cassette as a storage medium. The general idea to use the cassette for code storage was as simple as it was smart. The cassette tape was affordable, available, and sturdy, but it also had certain limitations as a material technology. For example, the procedure of recording broadcast code included a constant fiddling with recording volumes, interruptions and noise, and the correct angular relationship and gap between the record head and the magnetic tape. Nevertheless, the cassette was, during the 1980s, used in a number of interesting combinations with other media. These interplays, in many ways, foreground how peer-to-peer file sharing would emerge as an everyday practice.

## THEORY: INTERMEDIALITY AND THE LOGIC OF SHARING

As of now, public service broadcasting is arguably struggling with how to relate to digitally augmented conditions such as data retention and innovation (Andersson Schwarz & Palmås, 2013). Other pertinent issues for public service broadcasting concerns the public and private archiving of material and, more recently, streaming capabilities. It is interesting to note how *Datorernas värld*, in the mid 1980s, actively encouraged, and relied on, the recording and sharing of their broadcasts—something which has been a bit tricky for public service broadcasting to support due to copyright issues. *Datorernas värld* thereby promoted a sharing logic through a combination of various media forms, or intermediality.

Intermediality refers to the analysis of the relations between various media. The relations can be of many types, but they are active components of a broader culture of media production, consumption, and prosumption. The idea of intermediality can be traced far back in history (Rajewsky, 2005) and has a number of different connotations. We may refer to three general meanings of intermediality (Arvidson, Askander, Bruhn, & Führer, 2007). It may refer to multimedia such as image and music combined into a television show. Similar to the first meaning, but with emphasis on the modalities of consumption and production, it may also refer to a combination of the human senses. Most relevant for this article, it may refer to the connections, or networks, between media as societal conditions that co-emerge with mediated practices and innovations. An important distinction is that intermediality does not refer exclusively to converging media but also to a structural condition where the interplay between distinct media forms—that engender the old and the new, the digital and the analogue—allow for a travel of practices over various divergent media forms. In a time where interest in "zombie media" (Hertz & Parikka, 2012) is on the rise, this distinction is relevant. While a free flow of content over different media platforms is pertinent (Jenkins, 2006), a retention of the specificity of the components of these media platforms is equally critical (Hayles, 2004). Because media both transform practices and transform in itself, the ways in which performances travel over intermedial connections is of constant interest. The separation of the new from the old was perhaps always already an untenable distinction and the current media ecosystem makes this dichotomous split even harder to make. However, this does not entail an equalization of media capacities. Rather, the diversity of this ecosystem becomes increasingly highlighted as intermedial innovation progresses. Different media have different capacities to interface, to transform and to distribute information.

So, if intermediality is predominantly a material condition, the logic of sharing is the most vital part of its "cultural layer" (Manovich, 2001). Much like intermediality, sharing refers to a wide range of discrete yet associated practices. The sharing surge (McGee & Skågeby, 2004) enabled through social networks includes, most prominently, a mix of production and consumption performed via collaborative media (Löwgren & Reimer, 2013). While the term "sharing" has arguably gone through a process of resignification, where it has become ubiquitous and, perhaps, superfluous, it is also intensely salient in our contemporary media-saturated society. Sharing contains notions of both conviviality and individuality. On the one hand, networked individualism (Wellman et al., 2003) makes its mark through a constant public or semi-public sharing and directing of the details and impressions of our personal lives. Social media are used to update our current statuses, receive likes, and communicate in more-or-less real time. This societal encouragement to disclose the self has detriments (Fejes & Dahlstedt, 2012), but is nevertheless virtually ever-present. Notably, the need to obscure identities and intimate information results in a renewed interest in anonymity and content-driven, rather than identity-driven, communities online.

Interestingly, this can be seen as a step back, to earlier online services and sharing cultures. On the other hand, there is also a more communal sense of sharing, which emphasizes its convivial and structural aspects (Bakardjieva, 2004). Sharing economies, enabled by an intermedial infrastructure, are often connected to "noble" values of openness, trust, and even altruism. More recently, however, sharing has also been subject to a reification and resignification, where these noble values of the term have been used in marketing and branding for products and services that are implicitly more connected to values relating to the aggregation of social data, surveillance, and return on investment. This is inevitable, and the separation of "good" versus "evil" sharing creates a dimension where each situation must be evaluated according to relevant criteria. There is no doubt that there are aspects of sharing at large, which have had the capability of disrupting and changing the landscape of media prosumption. In fact, sharing is arguably the most central practice of our current media landscape (Snickars, 2012).

The theoretical combination of intermediality and sharing forms a simple socio-material framework from which we can address the specific capacities of media technologies in terms of how they support the central practice of sharing. We can trace how sharing can travel over intermedial networks, making new use of both people and machines. In other words, practices that are enabled by the logic of sharing make use of intermedial relations in order to "work," both for efficiency and for resilience, should structures collapse. These practices are multivocal, but not without power differentials. They include remediation, reappropriation, and a wide range of techno-cultural transformations.

## RESULTS

Let us reiterate the questions posed earlier: How did file sharing take place before the internet's mainstream usage, and how have the practices altered over time? My overall ambition is to reflect on the relationship between sociotechnical change and stasis. This relationship is complex, and defining something exclusively as a difference or a similarity can prove hard. While certain phenomena more obviously belong to one category rather than the other, there are also those that occupy an in-between space. For example, if many of the media technologies of this recent past (specifically cassettes and home computers) have been significantly marginalized, but now experience a revival as zombie media—is that best considered as change or stasis?

### Media Specificity

An interesting discussion concerns the different computer models included in the show, each one with its own processor and operating system. Therefore, all software that was transmitted would only run on some of the available home computers. A similar parallel can be made to the personal computer versus Macintosh distinction that created distinct realms of computing, though that border has become increasingly blurred in recent years. So, the broadcast programs were specific to one computer brand/model. This created a dilemma for the show, as it had limited airtime and also relied on the contributions of listeners. A potential solution to the skewing of broadcast programs was developed by the Dutch radio, which also ran a similar home computer code broadcast on its program *Hobbyscoop*. BASICODE was a multiplatform programming language which could be run on virtually all home computer models, created with the democratizing ambition to become the Esperanto of the computer world.

The producers of *Datorernas värld*, however, believed that, although the idea of a standard would be good for home computer owners in general, it also constituted a lowest common denominator that only supported the most basic functionality of a computer. Platform-specific capabilities, mainly relating to graphics and sound, could not be fully utilized. They thus made the decision to keep broadcasting platform-specific code even though this resulted in fewer executable programs for the individual listener. The media-specific analysis, as later suggested by Hayles (2004, 2008), becomes particularly salient in this example. BASICODE would have reduced the media-specificity of each computer model—a clear indication of the importance of analyzing how material capacities influence aesthetic expressions, programming potentials and interaction logic.

## Education and Folk Learning

Throughout the material, the significance of computer science education and programming was emphasized. Additionally, listeners were often encouraged to examine the broadcast source code, improve on it, and share those improvements. Sharing is here taken as an integral part of learning more about computational matters. As an ambition, this was clearly embryonic to the digital culture of sharing and open source code that is so prevalent today. While domestic, sneakernet-type sharing was well underway at the time, the objective of *Datorernas värld* was to expand the scope of the logic of sharing by making use of combinations of available media. As mentioned, the underlying context was primarily one of education and folk learning. The hosts mentioned that they selected which programs to broadcast depending on how well they stimulated popular interest in programming. Although the ambition to extend the spread of sharing was central, the show hosts maintained that their resources were limited. As such, they routinely emphasized the necessity of listeners to also engage locally, in a computer club, in order to get access to a more direct exchange of experiences and insights. The show hosts also underlined the growing importance of mediated communication, and listeners were encouraged to buy or rent a modem and start connecting to online databases. In general, the material reflected a spur of interest in computer-mediated communication and online resources. Many listeners correspondingly asked questions about which modems to use and which databases were the most useful. Modems, however, were quite expensive, which created a market for renting the necessary equipment. This parallels the introduction of other costly consumer technologies, such as the VCR.

Later on in the series, a growing range of dial-up databases were presented and reviewed, including a growing access to distance university courses. This led to an interesting tension in terms of learning. The more formal public approach, including online courses and organized computer clubs, appears to have happened in opposition to the self-organizing and informal networks and groups that emerged and engaged in sophisticated divisions of labor. An important question was whether this potential division between a more formalized, "serious" mode of learning through home computers and a more "rebellious" form should be connected to the division between "office computers" and "home computers." This separation was often made, both in the commercial material of the time, as well as by the editors of *Datorernas värld*. Nevertheless it proved a bit problematic since the border between them was often transgressed due to a quite tangible condition: cost.

Listeners' access to computers was a precondition for the educational ambition of *Datorernas värld*. Hobbyists and young enthusiasts required access to machines in order to learn about them. This access was often connected to parents' workplaces. A home computer was relatively expensive, and one way to circumvent this cost was to borrow or buy redundant computers from workplaces or schools. For example, the editors decided to broadcast more programs for the ABC80, a Swedish-made computer sold to schools, since it was increasingly regarded as outmoded at schools and was thereby transferred into households. Thus, the social change inherent to computer culture could be said to depend on or be driven by the benevolence and practical work of parents. Here, processes such as planned obsolescence and continuous updating would have come into play. The argument that home computer culture is partly built upon the residing potential in "outdated" technologies seems plausible (Acland, 2007). A similar contemporary parallel can be made to how children inherit their parents' obsolete smartphones, which are then put to new uses, most likely overlooked by their previous owners.

Another prevalent theme in discussions of learning and education was the anticipated transformation of kids and students from passive consumers to active producers. The computer was projected as a powerful way to make young pupils more engaged and more creative in processes of learning-through-making. Again, the discussion is familiar in relation to contemporaneous efforts.

Recent online projects such as codeacademy.com, code.org, hacking workshops for kids and the argument, pursued by academics, politicians, business leaders, and activists alike, that everyone should learn how to code (Rushkoff, 2010) clearly indicate that this is still a popular idea. However, it has also met with a significant amount of resistance. Detractors point to such things as a necessary division of labor (where coding skills are not crucial to all jobs), a potential decrease in the general quality of programmers (including a degree of celebration of the programmer as someone unique and extremely qualified) and a questioning of the causal connection between coding and general problem solving (i.e., there are still good and bad programmers). The detractors who were given voice in *Datorernas värld* were more concerned with how programmers and "screen personnel" would become the new blue-collar workers. Today, this discussion has expanded into theories of digital labor and playbor (Scholz, 2013) as exploitative of virtually all online activities.

## Surveillance, Personal Integrity, and Piracy

Surveillance and personal integrity were frequent topics in *Datorernas värld*, particularly the (potential) misplacing or misuse of data as a recurring issue. These issues are balanced by a continuous praising of the capabilities to store and to recall digitized information. Notably, when reporting on the use of personal information in databases the term "follow" is used in relation to tracing individuals through big data. While the term is generic, it is still interesting to see how it has a history in the early uses of databases for individual data mining. The show also discussed how computers aid in quantifying, measuring, and comparing human activities. Interestingly, these processes of rationalization are not always seen as beneficial to the individual. Again, a parallel can be made to contemporary discourses about the collection of personal information or the support for a "quantification of the self" through applications (apps) that record our behaviors and corporeal capacities. Another interesting detail is how *Datorernas värld* included a representative from the Swedish Data Inspection Board. This public official replied to listener questions and, for example, explained, or even defended, the storing of personal details in various archives.

The inclusion of a public authority figure to clarify things indicates a deep respect for policy and law. This is also clear when piracy is discussed. In virtually every show, the editors stressed the importance of contributors guaranteeing that they were the authors of the submitted programs, and that *Datorernas värld* had the express permission to broadcast them. This points to the peculiar position held by a public service company. The promotion of copying and sharing content has not been a prominent ambition of public service broadcasting. Still, *Datorernas värld* points to a growing importance of the sharing logic in new media landscapes. When it comes to piracy as the copying and sharing of commercial software, *Datorernas värld* mentioned that it is malicious and resulted in higher costs for development. However, they also mentioned how private copying was allowed and that it was only commercial re-selling that was prohibited by law. This distinction had effects on later discussions on large-scale file sharing. For example, many legal-technical debates emerged around the meaning of "copying on a limited scale" and what media that can be regarded as "specifically designed for private copying" (which are some of the phrasings used in legislation and policies). Naturally, a growing use of digital media and networking increasingly blurs these boundaries. Up until the time of *Datorernas värld*, however, the sharing logic was mainly limited to other formats and technologies such as video cassettes.

## Gender

It is hard to disregard how the sharing culture around *Datorernas värld* was profoundly masculinized. Of the 90 programs that were broadcast by *Datorernas värld* during 1985 and 1986, *all* were written and submitted by males. Several explanations can be offered for this fact. One of the most fundamental, but in a sense also most trivial, is that technology has become tightly coupled with masculinity. This was perhaps even more true at the time of home computer domestication, when skepticism toward computers and "computer nerds" was more commonplace (Nissen, 1993). It is, however, interesting to note how the marginalization of women in computing appears to have had a long history. It consists of different underpinnings than the current sexualization of content or fear of engaging in illegal activities that are sometimes given as explanations (Svensson, Larsson, & de Kaminski, 2014). Sexualization and criminalization are of course discouraging aspects of current file sharing cultures, but *Datorernas värld* points to the fact that computer expertise (Bassett, 2013) was, very early on, embraced and territorialized mainly by males.

## Intermediality

While the topics treated in *Datorernas värld* were interesting in themselves, there is also reason to consider the show from a media-material point of view. As such, *Datorernas värld* is clearly permeated by the theme of intermediality. With this in mind, the audiocassette, the home computer and the radio constitute a thought-provoking intermedial triad. In this interplay between media there are several relations worth examining, both as a historical curiosities, and as continuities or discontinuities in relation to our current media ecology. To further this idea, we may note that the cassette and the home computer would in fact interplay with an additional range of media and foreground several aspects of contemporary file sharing cultures. Taking the domestication of the home computer as a vantage point, an identification of a number of interesting areas of intermediality can be made, all with the audiocassette as a nodal point.

The ambition to popularize wireless file sharing was in many ways a historical meeting point for the sharing cultures and media convergences that later emerged. Sweden was not the only country—nor the first—to conduct such experiments. The Netherlands, Finland, Britain, and the German Democratic Republic all broadcast code over the air. Besides trying to document this era in media history, it is also important to analyze the interplay between media capacities and the concurrently emerging practices. As mentioned, a democratizing ambition arose around both folk education and the development of equalizing programming languages such as BASICODE.

The audiocassette enabled the selling, trading, and gifting of computer programs among users and was thereby an early social medium among home computer owners. Because it was a compact medium, it could also be sent through regular mail to more remote friends and acquaintances (Skågeby, 2011). Media research has examined the audiocassette as a medium in different social networks, but always with a focus on music or speech (Bijsterveld & Jacobs, 2009), not with a focus on computer code and its unique capability for holding multimedia content, and consequently this medium's role in the popularization of file sharing has been overlooked.

Because of the convenient size of the cassette, magazines and fanzines began to include it as part of their distribution. In Sweden, the fanzine *Joystick Computer Club* became a channel for the distribution of user-generated computer programs. Furthermore, commercial magazines also began to include cassettes with computer programs as added value, which indicates how file sharing has always carried a tension between the amateur and the professional, between consumer and producer and between commercial venture and hobby.

The fact that the cassette was a storage medium with rather limited bandwidth (transmission speed) led users to develop different forms of speed-increasing and compression software. As a general phenomenon, this demonstrates how the programmability of the computer became an important part of overcoming media limitations and the development of innovative digital problem solutions.

Apart from the audiocassette, the radio, and the home computer, there were also other but still related intermedial interactions touched upon in *Datorernas värld*. One program noted the increase in telephone traffic after a television program's broadcast. This observation was made in the context of bandwidth on telephone copper wires. The discussion concerned the communication infrastructure and how well (or ill) equipped it was to handle concurrent computer traffic. A comparison can be made with contemporary Twitter traffic in relation to, for example, the Oscar ceremony awards or a live sports event, again indicating interesting intermedial relations between existing and emerging media.

The file sharing culture we live in today certainly has a legacy in the interplay among media in the 1980s. The interaction that took place among home computers, cassette tapes, radio, and regular mail in a way predicted how media of today work: wirelessly, ubiquitously, through the blurring of consumption and production, and by interplay of analog and digital media.

## DISCUSSION AND CONCLUSION: SOCIOTECHNICAL CHANGE AND STASIS

The intermedial combination of public service broadcasting (PSB) and home computers in individual households in Sweden points to an interesting paradox in terms of push and pull. PSB is a form of centralized communication with its actual content selected by various editorial boards. At the same time, the very foundation of *Datorernas värld* was the active and contributing home computer owner or "peer" (Skågeby, 2011). A comparison can be made to the media ecology of today where a pull logic is ideologically promoted by many "information idealists" while at the same time, a commercial push logic is still dictating the consumption patterns on a large scale (Andersson Schwarz, 2013). The case of *Datorernas värld* actually prefigured how peer interaction and sharing often comes to rely on more centralized and controlled channels of communication. Today, this paradox has been scaled up. The commercial and regulated push logic of today is even more subtly infiltrating and resignifying the (assertedly) individual free choice of the pull logic. A timely example would be increasingly popular streaming media services, where the raw functions of fetching and acquiring content ("pull logic") are complemented by persuasive techniques of marketing and co-optation. Arguably, these consumption-based techniques are, in turn, cases of "evil by design" (Nodder, 2013), where a combined susceptibility of users and cold calculation of design(ers) allows companies to make us feel in control (and even good) while actually doing what they want.

The themes that were discussed in *Datorernas värld* seem fundamental to contemporary debates around computers in society. Privacy, piracy, online education, technostress, and artificial intelligence are still hot topics in the form of National Security Agency surveillance, pirate parties, massive open online courses, "media diets," and the singularity. However, there are also striking differences, particularly relating to the anticipated capacities of future technologies and the foreseen pace of development. The speculative extrapolation from what was the state-of-the-art of that time seems to rely on a logic of linear progression. In a parallel, but both larger and slightly more theoretical scale, many contemporary scholars correspondingly argue that there is no clear separation between new and old media. Rather, new media development is characterized by a continuous remediation of old media features, "a defining characteristic of the new digital media" (Bolter & Grusin, 2000, p. 45). According to remediation theory, the old is always visible in the new. From a media-archeological perspective it is, however, equally important to look for the new in the old (Zielinski, 2006). As such, media-archeological studies can be said to have two general aims: to study the motives and features that are currently reused in media development, and to study how these discourses have materialized as media technologies and systems in specific historical contexts (Huhtamo, 1995).

When considering *digital* media it becomes important to recognize the capacity of computer code to represent all other media (Berry, 2011; Murray, 2012). While coding was early on a skill limited to professional programmers, the increasingly affordable home computer and the mobile storage media that came with it enabled a new practice: file sharing. As such, the sharing of code—and thereby also the increased possibilities to learn about coding—introduced programming to new breed of consumers. The education system was quick to pick up on the topic area, but has arguably been less successful in realizing it in actual teaching and learning. As demonstrated, there is now a significant boost in popularity relating to advocacy for public coding skills.

The triad of home computer, audiocassette, and radio constitutes an intermission, where both preceding and succeeding intermedialities will have to be charted. The cassette was gradually made obsolete as a storage medium for home computing, replaced by the floppy disk. Apart from the floppy disk, which generated its own distinctive practices such as designed covers and attached letters, a range of intermedial relations and connected practices also emerged. A few that are worthy of academic attention include ASCII graphics; the division of labor in demos; crack intros (Reunanen, Wasiak, & Botz, in press); copy parties; and commercials and advertisements about home computers. Still, a mapping needs to begin somewhere, and beginning "in the middle" is inevitable as the timelines that intersect in media archaeological studies are intricate. Old media may show how certain practices may have existed for a long time, without having been realized or reaching a critical user mass. New media become old, but old media are also revived in different ways. "Dead" media become "zombie" media. All media were new (at least in a practical sense and to the public) when they were introduced. As such, it is a good idea to go back before the hype and revisit, or even revive, dead, forgotten and/or obscured media in an effort to understand not only what is new about new media, but also what is old about new media and what is new about old media (Huhtamo & Parikka, 2011). As such, the media archaeology of piracy would be a particularly interesting project for the future. For example, through researching the various cloned computer models (e.g., the pirated Lemon, Orange, Peach and Pineapple versions of the Apple II) and other media technologies and programs that were developed (e.g., in Singapore, Hong Kong, and Taiwan), a parallel history of development and usage could be charted. When it comes to the media archaeology of file sharing, there are some studies and projects underway, but it remains fairly unexamined from an academic perspective. The point in time when computers entered the home, and the intermedial practices which emerged with that domestication, is an exciting and relevant point of reference. The interplay between home computer, audiocassette, and radio broadcasting illustrates how productive synergies between established media and new media can emerge.

## REFERENCES

Acland, C. R. (Ed.). (2007). *Residual media*. Minneapolis, MN: University of Minnesota Press.
Andersson Schwarz, J. (2013). *Online file sharing: Innovations in media consumption*. London, England: Routledge.
Andersson Schwarz, J., & Palmås, K. (2013). Introducing the panspectric challenge: A reconfiguration of regulatory values in a multiplatform media landscape. *Central European Journal of Communication*, 6(2), 219–233.
Arvidson, J., Askander, M., Bruhn, J., & Führer, H. (Eds.). (2007). *Changing borders: Contemporary positions in intermediality* (Vol. 1). Lund, Sweden: Intermedia Studies Press.
Bakardjieva, M. (2004). Virtual togetherness: An everyday life perspective. In A. Feenberg & D. Barney (Eds.), *Community in the digital age: Philosophy and practice*. New York, NY: Rowman & Littlefield.
Bassett, C. (2013). Feminism, expertise and the computational turn. In H. Thornham & E. Weissmann (Eds.), *Renewing feminisms: Radical narratives, fantasies and futures in media studies* (pp. 199–214). London, England: I.B. Tauris.
Berry, D. M. (2011). *The philosophy of software: Code and mediation in the digital age*. Basingstoke, England: Palgrave MacMillan.
Bijsterveld, K., & Jacobs, A. (2009). Storing sound souvenirs: The multi-sited domestication of the tape recorder. In K. Bijsterveld & J. van Dijck (Eds.), *Sound souvenirs: Audio technologies, memory and cultural practices* (pp. 25–42). Amsterdam, The Netherlands: Amsterdam University Press.
Bolter, J. D., & Grusin, R. (2000). *Remediation: Understanding new media*. Cambridge, MA: MIT Press.
Fejes, A., & Dahlstedt, M. (2012). *The confessing society: Foucault, confession and practices of lifelong learning*. London, England: Routledge.
Hanspach, M., & Goetz, M. (2013). On covert acoustical mesh networks in air. *Journal of Communications*, 8(11), 758–767.
Hayles, N. K. (2004). Print is flat, code is deep: The importance of media-specific analysis. *Poetics Today*, 25(1), 67–90.
Hayles, N. K. (2008). The materiality of informatics: Audiotape and its cultural niche. In B. Highmore (Ed.), *The design culture reader* (pp. 317–327). London, England: Routledge.
Hertz, G., & Parikka, J. (2012). Zombie media: Circuit bending media archaeology into an art method. *Leonardo*, 45(5), 424–430.
Huhtamo, E. (1995). Resurrecting the technological past: An introduction to the archaeology of media art. *InterCommunication*, 14, 2.
Huhtamo, E., & Parikka, J. (Eds.). (2011). *Media archaeology: Approaches, applications, and implications*. Berkeley, CA: University of California Press.
Jenkins, H. (2006). *Convergence culture: Where old and new media collide*. New York, NY: New York University Press.
Kraftwerk. (1981). *Computerwelt*. [CD]. Düsseldorf, Germany: Kling Klang.
Lasar, M. (2012, August 19). Experiments in airborne BASIC—"buzzing" computer code over FM radio. *ars technica*.
Löwgren, J., & Reimer, B. (2013). *Collaborative media: Production, consumption and design interventions*. Cambridge, MA: MIT Press.
Manovich, L. (2001). *The language of new media*. Cambridge, MA: MIT Press.
Marks, P. (2013, November 14). Can a computer virus communicate via your speakers? *New Scientist*. Retrieved from http://www.newscientist.com/article/dn24582-can-a-computer-virus-communicate-via-your-speakers. html#.VKkN9yetzNU
McGee, K., & Skågeby, J. (2004). Gifting technologies. *First Monday*, 9(12).

Murray, J. H. (2012). *Inventing the medium: Principles of interaction design as a cultural practice*. Cambridge, MA: MIT Press.

Nissen, J. (1993). *Pojkarna vid datorn: Unga entusiaster i datateknikens värld*. (PhD), Symposion Graduale, Stockholm/Stehag.

Nodder, C. (2013). *Evil by design: Interaction design to lead us into temptation*. Indianapolis, IN: John Wiley & Sons.

Parikka, J. (2010, October 1). What is media archaeology?—beta definition 0.8. Cartographies of media archaeology [Web log post]. Retrieved from http://mediacartographies.blogspot.se/2010/10/what-is-media-archaeology-beta.html

Parikka, J. (2012). *What is media archaeology?* Malden, MA: Polity Press.

Rajewsky, I. O. (2005). Intermediality, intertextuality, and remediation: A literary perspective on intermediality. *intermédialités*, *6*, 43–64.

Reunanen, M., Wasiak, P., & Botz, D. (in press). Crack intros: Piracy, creativity and communication. *International Journal of Communication*.

Rushkoff, D. (2010). *Program or be programmed: Ten commands for a digital age*. New York, NY: OR Books.

Scholz, T. (Ed.). (2013). *Digital labor: The internet as playground and factory*. New York, NY: Routledge.

Skågeby, J. (2008). *Gifting technologies: Ethnographic studies of end-users and social media sharing*. (Doctoral dissertation). Linköping University, Linköping.

Skågeby, J. (2011). Slow and fast music media: Comparing values of cassettes and playlists. *Transformations Journal of Media & Culture*, *20*. Retrieved from http://www.transformationsjournal.org/journal/issue_20/article_04.shtml

Snickars, P. (2012). *A force like no other: Digitization, culture, media*. Paper presented at the Truly Digital Conference, Stockholm, Sweden.

Svensson, M., Larsson, S., & de Kaminski, M. (2014). The research bay—studying the global file sharing community. In W. T. Gallagher & D. Halbert (Eds.), *Law and society perspectives on intellectual property law*. Cambridge, England: Cambridge University Press.

Wellman, B., Quan-Haase, A., Boase, J., Chen, W., Hampton, K., Isla de Diaz, I., & Miyata, K. (2003). The social affordances of the internet for networked individualism. *Journal of Computer-mediated Communication*, *8*(3).

Zielinski, S. (2006). *Deep time of the media: Toward an archaeology of hearing and seeing by technical means*. Cambridge, MA: MIT Press.

# Anonymous and the Political Ethos of Hacktivism

Luke Goode

*University of Auckland*

This article examines the ethos of the hacktivist movement Anonymous. It considers the subcultural roots of Anonymous and the political and ethical values articulated by the movement. The article highlights key points of tension within the Anonymous ethos: nihilism and idealism, utopianism and dystopianism, individualism and collectivism, and negative and positive liberty. The article argues that while Anonymous can be broadly understood as cyberlibertarian, it is more complex and contradictory than this singular label implies. However, it also argues that the Anonymous ethos is not so amorphous that it prevents ideological analysis and critique. The article concludes by discussing the wider political significance of Anonymous when seen in this light.

## INTRODUCTION

This article examines the ethos of the hacktivist movement Anonymous. It considers its subcultural roots and the political and ethical values articulated by the movement. In particular, the paper draws attention to key points of tension within the Anonymous ethos: nihilism and idealism, utopianism and dystopianism, individualism and collectivism, and negative and positive liberty. Existing literature provides varying assessments of hacktivist values. One perspective portrays Anonymous specifically (Coleman, 2011a, p. 511) and hacktivism more generally (Liu, 2004, pp. 361–367) as essentially fluid or "rhizomatic" and thus resistant to stable ideological categories. Another perspective identifies hacktivist movements such as Anonymous with "information anarchism" and libertarian values (Jordan, 2008, p. 77). A further perspective sees Anonymous reflecting liberal ideology while containing seeds of a socialist worldview (Fuchs, 2013). This article aims not to reject any of these perspectives but rather to add a complementary one. Characterizing Anonymous as ostensibly libertarian or, specifically, cyberlibertarian (see Golumbia, 2013) is valuable but underplays ideological complexities and tensions within the movement. Emphasizing the movement's rhizomatic and shape-shifting qualities, though, risks understating some clearly identifiable political and moral positions of the movement. This article seeks to complement existing scholarship navigating between both analytical poles, suggesting that Anonymous is too complex for a singular ideological label such as "cyberlibertarian" but not so amorphous that it prevents ideological analysis and critique.

This article offers a theoretical analysis drawing on secondary literature, but also on popular sources containing testimony from Anonymous participants—these serve as primary texts for critical analysis. These texts (a book-length collection of reflections by Anonymous members, a journalistic book documenting the movement, and a documentary film) illustrate a series of tensions or oppositions within the movement's political ethos. They do not grant direct access to the movement in the way that ethnographies can, but have the virtue of highlighting a breadth and diversity of Anonymous voices, and of presenting those voices in a more reflective and less strategic mode compared with the study of Anonymous' own campaign videos. Again, the aim is not to question the validity of these other approaches or data sources but rather to provide a complementary perspective.

Here the term "ethos" is drawn from political theory to indicate not only expressed political and ethical values but also the behavior, character, and disposition of individual political actors (Heclo, 2003), groups, or institutions (Diamond, 1986, pp. 77–78). It also describes attitudes towards political institutions and processes (Wilson & Banfield, 1971). Finally, "political ethos" refers also to "politicized sentiments" (Jenkins, 1991, p. 141); this underscores how moral and political values are bound up with emotions including passions and resentments. As such, the term ethos (rather than ethics or values) is deployed to include emotional as well as moral and political registers of Anonymous.

The article first provides some background to Anonymous including its roots, tactics, and values. It then moves to a critical analysis of the movement's ethos, first by unpacking the term cyberlibertarian as a descriptor for Anonymous, and then through the framework of key binary oppositions (nihilism/idealism; utopia/dystopia; individualism/collectivism; positive/negative liberty). It concludes by discussing the broader political significance of Anonymous in light of this analysis.

## ANONYMOUS AND HACKTIVISM

The term "hacktivist," commonly applied to Anonymous, combines computer hacking and activism. For Anonymous, the hacker subculture preceded the activism, in common with another well-known hacker group Cult of the Dead Cow (cDc) established in the 1980s, and in contrast to another, the Electronic Disturbance Theater (hacking in support of the Zapatistas) for whom hacking was always a political tool. Anonymous and cDc also shared a notorious target, the Church of Scientology. We should not overstate the groups' similarities: cDc members have, for example, criticized tactics deployed by Anonymous such as defacing or taking down websites as hypocritical attacks on free speech (Allnut, 2011). But both groups share a sense that computer technology is more than *just* a tool for achieving political ends (Taylor, 2005, p. 46). The ethos of Anonymous is technophilic and digital technology is heralded not only as a way of life for group members but also as a driving force for reshaping society.

The term hacktivist, apart from giving the false impression that computer hacking is the only weapon in Anonymous's arsenal (which includes street protests, media campaigns, and distributed denial of service, or DDoS, attacks which are not strictly hacks), also fails to capture how Anonymous' roots lie beyond hacking and activism in the online subculture of the 4chan image board, particularly in subdomain /b/. Founded in 2003 by American teenager Chris Poole, 4chan was little known beyond its participants until its recent notoriety thanks to Anonymous.

90

Conceived initially as forum for anime, it came to specialize in adolescent "gross-out" content, pornography, and politically incorrect humor. It became a carnivalesque celebration of free speech through the transgression of conventions and taboos around depictions of violence and sex. 4chan was also an incubator for now ubiquitous memes such as lolcats: 4chan juxtaposed innocuous and cutesy with extreme and intentionally offensive material (Knuttila, 2011; Stryker, 2011). Participants were either anonymous or pseudonymous, but a joke idea of "Anon" as a singular identity caught on and the beginnings of Anonymous took root. 4chan was a rowdy place, and tension flared especially between those who embraced collective anonymity and those who cultivated pseudonymous identities, the latter disparaged by the former as "namefags." Politically incorrect language was and remains a hallmark: 4chan and Anonymous members routinely trade homophobic, racist and misogynistic language. The degree to which the idioms of 4chan and Anonymous correlate with racist, misogynistic, or homophobic *attitudes* is questionable (Olson, 2013, p. 411)—participants often claim the language is, instead, a subversive performance of incivility.

Anonymous hacktivism emerged at the intersection of pranksterism, or "trolling," and reaction against institutional practices perceived to impinge on the sanctity of free speech: "I came for the lulz but stayed for the outrage" as one of ethnographer Gabriella Coleman's respondents put it (2011b, p. 3). The Church of Scientology's attempt in 2008 to suppress a leaked video of Tom Cruise talking in rapturous and incoherent terms about the religion sparked a huge reaction. This began with mockery of Scientology's naïve disregard for the "Streisand effect," whereby attempts to suppress content simply fuel its circulation and notoriety. It evolved into a more serious (though never humorless) battle against an exploitative, wealthy, and powerful cult, energizing existing Anons and attracting new ones. The "Chanology" campaign was waged online (DDoS attacks), via phone and fax (prank calls and black faxes) and on the streets. Anonymous would later target a smaller but ideologically more noxious religious cult, the Westbro Baptist Church. Other high profile campaigns were waged against private computer security firm HBGary in 2011 (in direct retaliation against the firm's boastful but erroneous claims about outing—or "dOxing"—Anonymous members), and PayPal, Visa and Mastercard in 2010 after they disabled donation facilities for Wikileaks, allegedly under pressure from US authorities. "Operation Payback" targeted the Motion Picture Association of America (MPAA) and the Recording Industry Association of America (RIAA) in retaliation for attempts to take down file-sharing site the Pirate Bay. In 2010 "Operation Titstorm" targeted the Australian government in response to its proposed mandatory internet pornography filter (Kravets, 2010). Anonymous tends to treat pornography, controversially, as a straightforward free speech issue. Moreover, it shared with other interest groups the view that a filter ostensibly targeting child pornography would be a "slippery slope" toward broader internet censorship—as one Anon remarks: "However abhorrent I might find these things, even more abhorrent is the idea that someone else can tell me what I can and can't look at" (Anonymous, 2013, p. 128).

Anonymous splinter group LulzSec targeted broadcaster PBS in 2011 after it aired *Wikisecrets*, a documentary the group perceived as biased against Wikileaks and Julian Assange (PBS, 2011). *The Sun* newspaper in the United Kingdom was hacked in the same year in response to the phone hacking scandal at Rupert Murdoch's News International. These LulzSec hacks undercut an established Anonymous convention against targeting media organizations, a principle designed to avert hypocritical attacks on free expression. 2011 also saw the infamous hack (now under the banner of "AntiSec") on global corporation Stratfor (Norton, 2011). Latterly Anonymous (stung by various arrests and convictions in the United States and United Kingdom during 2011) has participated in actions alongside Occupy groups and assisted in leaking documents associated with the Edward Snowden/NSA scandal. It also provided assistance and guidance to protesters in Tunisia and then other countries involved in the Arab Spring who faced censorship, surveillance and crack-downs on dissidents. More recently, Anonymous has attacked copyright institutions, including the RIAA and MPAA, in the wake of debates around the controversial Stop Online Piracy Act (SOPA) and the shutdown of file locker service MegaUpload and extradition proceedings against its founder Kim Dotcom on piracy charges. In 2013, Anonymous members attacked the Department of Justice in the wake of indicted internet activist Aaron Swartz's suicide (Limer, 2013).

Anonymous tactics range from simple DDoS and botnet attacks, website defacement, and social engineering (tricking people into revealing security details), through to sophisticated hacking, locating, and exploiting security vulnerabilities and breaching large organizations' information technology networks. Tactics are commonly mixed within particular "Ops." DDoS attacks work on scale: large numbers of people (requiring few technical skills) use simple software to overwhelm a site with traffic. This method is inclusive, fostering a sense of community, yet also commonly disparaged for limited effectiveness, for crudeness, and for landing too many unwitting young adults on the wrong side of the law. Botnets hijack remote computers (unbeknownst to their owners) to attack a target, and control of botnets is a source of elite status among Anons (Olson, 2013). (Elite status entails operatives using consistent pseudonyms over time, suggesting the group's name is a partial misnomer: anonymity, pseudonymity, and sometimes real-world identities co-exist within the movement.) Website defacements allowed Anonymous to develop its brand identity: simple black and white imagery and text, righteous and foreboding language (designed to unsettle targets and to amuse those in the know). LulzSec hacks adopted a more explicitly pranksterish tone: a spoofed report of Tupac Shakur turning up alive in New Zealand appeared on PBS online (Markoff, 2011) and *The Sun*'s website revealed Rupert Murdoch had taken his own life in the wake of the phone hacking scandal (Arthur, 2011).

Anonymous has also been fertile ground for hackers to showcase both technical and social engineering skills. Hacker culture is imbued with a meritocratic and competitive ethos whereby hackers and security experts seek to outdo each other (Levy, 2010, pp. 32–33). The classic if simplistic distinction in hacker culture is between legitimate "white hats" (hackers hired to locate security vulnerabilities) and "black hats" or "crackers" with malevolent motives. "Gray hats" execute unauthorized hacks with a benign motive to expose security flaws, though reputation and status may also be at stake (Bozzo, 2009). Anonymous, however, does not quite fit this typology. Detractors may view them as black hats, while the longer-term, if unintended, consequences of their actions may be more like gray hat hacking—unauthorized hacks resulting ultimately in their target organizations enhancing security. Nonetheless they differ in their overtly moral and political motives. Anonymous's roots are essentially prepolitical: the movement emerged from a subculture dedicated to "lulz" and poking fun at authority (hence pre- rather than apolitical), but a more serious political purpose emerged with battles against powerful and corrupt governmental, corporate, and religious interests. Indeed, a fault-line opened up within the movement as some wished to keep the actions focused on lulz and pranks and disparaged as "moralfags" those who pursued a more overtly political and moral purpose. The following sections examine this purpose more systematically, first through the lens of cyberlibertarianism.

## POLITICS OF ANONYMOUS

David Golumbia claims that Anonymous is a cyberlibertarian entity (2013, p. 16). Cyberlibertarianism, a term emerging in the 1990s, reflects the prevailing philosophy of the hackers and technology entrepreneurs responsible for developing the internet and for defending it from government regulation (Borsook, 2000; Naughton, 2000). Cyberlibertarianism lives on today through organizations such as the Electronic Frontier Foundation (EFF), campaigns against the expansion of digital copyright regimes, and various (though not all) pro-piracy and anti-surveillance campaigns. Golumbia defines cyberlibertarianism broadly as faith in the capacity for unconstrained progress in digital technology to solve social problems including inequality of opportunity, shortcomings in the democratic process, and unequal access to knowledge and education. "Unconstrained" in this context actually means directed by market principles, with governments keeping out of a domain they are perceived neither to understand nor to have the capacity to control. Technology, like the market, is viewed as a complex emergent phenomenon, prone to the Hayekian "fatal conceit." A classic statement of cyberlibertarianism is John Perry Barlow's (1996) *Declaration of the Independence of Cyberspace.* There is also a strong strain of technological determinism within cyberlibertarianism. This can be expressed fatalistically in terms of a "new reality" (for better or worse) dictated by the juggernaut of technological progress: governments, corporations, and individuals must simply adapt or perish. Alvin Toffler's *Future Shock* (1970) and *The Third Wave* (1980) are classic touchstones. This position echoes the *economic* fatalism of neoliberal ideology and Margaret Thatcher's notorious TINA doctrine ("there is no alternative"). Technological determinism can also be expressed in more utopian and technophilic terms: techno-utopians including George Gilder and *Wired* magazine have evangelized for a technologically-driven world of rational markets, free individuals and post-ideological politics.

Golumbia argues that cyberlibertarianism deploys an exclusively negative conception of freedom—freedom to act without constraint so long as one avoids constraining the freedom of others (ironically the Hayekian conceit is smuggled back in here, as if impacts on others were transparent, direct and measurable), and neglects and even disparages positive conceptions of freedom such as support for government policies placing universal access requirements on telecoms companies or regulation of online hate speech. While Golumbia's essay raises useful questions, assigning the cyberlibertarian tag wholesale to a diversity of individuals and institutions is limiting: to suggest Jimmy Wales (Wikipedia founder and professed Randian), Julian Assange (of Wikileaks), Lawrence Lessig (Creative Commons founder), and Mark Zuckerberg (Facebook chief executive officer) are all cut from the same ideological cloth represents a rather blunt analysis of their respective statements and actions. More importantly here, though, Golumbia's attribution of the label to Anonymous begs further questions.

It is true that cyberlibertarianism and the hacker ethic are almost of a piece. Steven Levy (2010, pp. 27–38) outlines the following core principles of hacker culture: "All information should be free" (often rendered anthropomorphically as "information *wants* to be free"); "Mistrust authority—promote decentralization" (a libertarian euphemism for "trust markets, not governments"); "Hackers should be judged by their hacking, not bogus criteria such as degrees, age, race, or position"; "Computers can change your life for the better" (elsewhere in Levy's book this principle morphs into the promise of a better *world* thanks to computers). Such principles clearly resonate with many Anons. This is especially clear in a number of recent media texts featuring testimony from Anonymous participants. While the campaign videos that have largely served as the public face of Anonymous hyperbolize and even ironize its message, these texts feature some of the voices behind the Anonymous mask in a more reflective vein, at arm's length from the crossfire of Ops and media publicity (though of course they are not free from mediation and performativity). In Brian Knappenberger's (2012) documentary *We Are Legion: The Story of the Hacktivists,* we hear from a range of influential, if second tier, Anons. Journalist Parmy Olson's *We Are Anonymous* (2013) fleshes out some of the backstories and motives of key participants (including the infamous "Topiary," aka Jake Davis, who was subsequently arrested and convicted by UK authorities). And a book of unedited submissions from unnamed Anons, published in the United Kingdom—*Anonymous on Anonymous* (2013)—is a polyvocal collage of ideas, reflections, dialogues, manifestos, and essays (some repurposed from other sources) lacking a singular narrative or explanatory framework but providing insight into participants' beliefs, motivations and aspirations. What these texts collectively suggest is that trying to fit Anonymous into an ideological box labeled cyberlibertarian (however broadly conceived) is problematic, implying a degree of coherence and common purpose that is less convincing on closer inspection.

In what follows I draw on these testimonial sources as I trace some of the ideological and ethical threads running through Anonymous. I aim to show how the movement's ethos can be characterized as a series of tensions. Most political and social movements contain ideological, cultural, or social tensions. These may be productive, adding strength and dynamism (conservationists and clean technology advocates coexisting within the Green movement, for example), or they may be more troublesome fault lines (even fatal contradictions) threatening a movement's vitality and durability (the difficulty with which social democratic parties balance working and middle class interests, for example). It is not possible to say conclusively whether the tensions within Anonymous discussed below are productive or counterproductive. But I will go on to suggest that they impact any assessment of the movement's wider political significance. I will suggest that the voices articulated through these testimonial texts are simultaneously nihilistic and idealistic, dystopian and utopian, egoistic and collectivist, and dedicated to the negative freedoms of libertarianism yet also concerned with collectivist goals of equality and justice.

## NIHILISM/IDEALISM

4chan has always reveled in nihilistic humor (participants have even debated nihilism philosophically via Nietzsche and Leo Strauss) and the nihilistic impulse has continued to reverberate through Anonymous. Critics and adherents alike have noted it: former NSA chief Michael Hayden lambasted the group as nihilists, akin to al-Qaida, (Ackerman, 2013), and a disaffected former member lamented a *decline* of nihilism and the ascendency of the "moralfags" (Greenberg, 2011). A full page in *Anonymous on Anonymous* is given over to an (unattributed) quote from artist Sam Durant: "I don't believe in nothing—I feel like they ought to burn down the world—just let it burn down" (Anonymous, 2013, p. 169). In the same publication, though, nihilistic sentiment jostles with images of Che Guevara and the clenched fist symbol of resistance, quotes on the romantic spirit of rebellion from HL Mencken, and of course references to the romantic anti-hero Guy Fawkes. Nihilism and romantic idealism are twin sides of a coin (unsurprisingly, two millennial movies—the nihilistic *Fight Club* [1999] and the idealistic *The Matrix* [1999]—are the most commonly invoked). The conjunction of nihilistic and idealistic impulses is hardly unique in youth-based subcultures and protest movements. The countercultural and protest movements of the late 1960s, for example, gave rise to both flower power and the militant Baader-Meinhof insurgents; it was a movement inspired both by Marcuse's libidinal manifesto *Eros and Civilization* (1955) *and* by his far more dismal diagnosis in *One Dimensional Man* (1964), which invoked a nihilistic movement of Great Refusal. Popular readings of Nietzsche (folk-hero of many countercultural movements) are similarly caught between nihilistic interpretations and a life-affirming and idealistic emphasis on the "transvaluation of values" (Nietzsche, 1968). While nihilistic attitudes are commonly disparaged as fatalistic, juvenile and even dangerous, the nihilism of Anonymous can be seen in the contemporary climate as an outlet for frustration toward the apparent lack of alternative visions that might challenge current political, social, and economic systems.

But Anonymous does not stop at simple nihilism. Echoes of Dada, the Situationist International and, in a more recent vein, culture jammers such as the Yes Men manifest in the antics and desire for spectacle and spoofing. We see a simultaneous critique *and* embrace of the absurd which, in existentialist philosophy, is closely linked to nihilism as mockery of conventional values. Trolling in its most playful (as opposed to vengeful) form is a kind of online absurdism. The absurd was on display at the Chanology protests (signs reading "honk if you're in a car" and "don't worry—we're from the internet" for example). Absurd spectacle characterized the LulzSec attacks on PBS and News International. Some of Anonymous' tactics can be understood as a kind of détournement (hijacking and altering websites and misappropriating proprietary data) and reaction against the recuperation (another concept in situationism) of information and culture through copyright regimes and state and corporate surveillance systems.

Nihilism and idealism coexist within the Anonymous ethos. This duality also features strongly in the history of anarchism (Marshall, 2008). While Coleman (2011c) has persuasively cautioned against overstating affinities between Anonymous and anarchism, *Anonymous on Anonymous*, with an emphasis on voices from Anonymous UK and in the wake of both Occupy and British government austerity, contains strong anarchist sentiments, underscored by punk "zine" aesthetics. The term "idealistic" is used here in both its everyday and philosophical senses: romantic or even righteous attachment to principles *and* belief in the power of ideas (more so than of material factors) to shape history. This second sense manifests in the commonplace assertion by participants that Anonymous is not a material entity or institution but merely "an idea" (Anonymous, 2013, p. 182). Topiary's final tweet prior to his arrest read "You cannot arrest an idea." Coleman (n.d.) has referred to Anonymous simply as "a cluster of ideals." The potency of "ideas" that transcend particular identities or interests has been underscored in recent times by, for example, the Occupy Movement whose biggest legacy, perhaps, has been to alter the discourse of contemporary politics by entrenching the idea of the 99%: here, the power of an idea is very tangible. To a lesser degree, Anonymous, too, has helped entrench the idea of "the internet" as an anonymous but powerful "we" demanding freedom from interference and encroachment by government or big business.

Yet the anonymity of the idea may obscure the interests behind it. Olson's (2013) journalistic account of Anonymous usefully reveals participants as real, embodied people, many living challenging or fractured lives, and Knappenberger's documentary (2012) provides visual embodiment: predominantly young white male protagonists. While this reinforces a hacker stereotype (socially awkward boys joke about meeting "hot girls" and "getting laid" after the Scientology protests), elsewhere Anons confront that stereotype. "Many still see this movement as solely a loose-knit group of hackers, young anarchic geeks. It is NOT," says one contributor to *Anonymous on Anonymous*: "I am, for instance, a 60-year-old woman who would not have a clue of how to hack into a computer" (Anonymous, 2013, p. 54). Embodied identities do matter, then, and the group's rhetorical idealism, including its meritocratic ethos and aspiration to disregard status, can serve as a mystification as well as an insight into its ideals. As an example, the influential *Hacker Manifesto*, penned in 1986 by "The Mentor," aka Loyd Blankenship (a white male hacker), is published in full in *Anonymous on Anonymous*, declaring: "We [hackers] exist without skin color, without nationality, without religious bias" (cited in Anonymous, 2013, p. 146).

There is idealism in the everyday sense, too, as participants commonly express faith in the movement through righteous language: "We do not forgive. We do not forget. Expect us," runs the tagline of numerous Anonymous videos and publications; "We see, we judge" declares another (p. 6). Such righteousness may often be laced with irony, but it is doubtful it can be characterized as *merely* ironic. Throughout *Anonymous on Anonymous*, for example, quasi-religious zeal is evident. Anonymous is referred to as a "creed": "Those who follow the creed are Anonymous. Those who make the attaining of knowledge their highest priority, are of the collective" (p. 180) states one Anon, hinting at a kind of spiritual enlightenment attainable through discipline and focus. "For me, been [sic] anonymous is like being born again," states another (p. 135). Another talks of the collective "radiat[ing] justice unto others" (p. 183). Others talk of an "awakening," a "fog clearing," a "journey down a rabbit hole" (p. 148) with echoes of *The Matrix* but also reminiscent of a religious cult: "All your life you have known that something is not right with this world. You can FEEL it in your heart. We all can. Anonymous are here to re-align the people with the truth" (p. 8); "Since I was a kid, I've always suspected that the world I existed in was fake, shallow and an illusion, but never had the knowledge to understand what was wrong . . . And now Anonymous is my home" (p. 37). This shades from the personal into the political: "Our great movement [is] the only one that has brought hope to millions of world citizens after one century of complete despair" (p. 124); and messages of solidarity with Iranian protestors are intoned with a rather priestly mix of support and rebuke: "To those that would remain intimidated into subdued silence: You have passively enabled your government to make a mockery of your freedom. Now is your chance for action, for redemption . . . A new dawn is approaching, that will set you and your great country free from the shackles of oppression, tyranny and torture. It will let you exhale, and finally take the first breath that will fill your lungs with strength, wisdom and freedom" (p. 134). These pious tones could be dismissed simply as humorous echoes of films such as *V for Vendetta* and *The Matrix* that have inspired Anons, or as ironic gestures. But their prevalence in these testimonial texts (and especially *Anonymous on Anonymous*) suggests in fact strong and sincere attachment to the movement's ideals.

## UTOPIA/DYSTOPIA

Anonymous rhetoric also oscillates between utopian and dystopian registers. Utopianism is conveyed through technophilic sentiments: a section in *Anonymous on Anonymous* entitled "We love the internet" waxes lyrical on the "awesome things it gives us" (2013, p. 22) and tells us we ("even the impoverished") are richer than "the richest Pharaohs of Ancient Egypt" for the ability to "hear the voice of a loved one from . . . the other side of the planet" (p. 34). But the internet is also seen to harbor a potential dystopia characterized by systematic surveillance and censorship

(p. 34). In this vein, Anons see themselves "surfing the waves of history" (Knappenberger, 2012), proclaiming that we are at a historical crossroads. Utopia and dystopia are best conceived not as irreconcilable opposites but as twin elements in a mode of thinking that opposes the strictures of pragmatic realism (see, e.g., Gordin, Tilley, & Prakash, 2010, pp. 1–3). Both are commonly disparaged as unrealistic at best and dangerous at worst, but may also be indispensable in creative and critical thinking about the present and the future (Levitas, 2010), especially in the contemporary political climate where "there is no alternative" doctrine prevails despite chronic social, geopolitical, economic and environmental crises (see Fisher, 2009).

The dystopian symbolism of Anonymous (the masks and the foreboding messages of impending judgment) is reflected in member testimony: "We live in a time that far surpasses George Orwell's nightmarish vision of *Nineteen Eight-Four* and hurtle toward an even more hellish future. This future, the New World Order, is desired by only the power hungry tiny minority on top of the pyramid. For the rest of us, potentially destined to be bound in abject slavery, life will not be worth living" (Anonymous, 2013, p. 54). But dystopian thinking can also be a pretext for utopianism and the same Anon continues: "I genuinely consider the movement to be one which will continue gather [sic] enough force to be instrumental in steering humanity away from the future . . . We are racing against time . . . . but I have faith . . . . . . . WE WILL SUCCEED!!!!" (p. 55). Coleman (2012, p. 86) sees in Anonymous the kind of utopian impulse theorized by Ernst Bloch—not wildly optimistic and totalizing blueprints but the presence and resilience of hope and "wishful thinking" embedded in fragments of everyday and popular culture, even amid a general atmosphere of despair or resignation (Bloch, 1986). But while Bloch defended "wishful thinking," he also delineated *mere* wishful thinking or "abstract utopianism" (which consoles and pacifies) from wishful thinking containing the seeds of a plausible movement for change, a "concrete utopia." A movement emphasizing the power of ideas above all else may, then, be prone to abstract utopianism.

## INDIVIDUALISM/COLLECTIVISM

Another polarity is individualism versus a spirit of collective endeavor. Egoistic concerns are reflected in the sanctification of free speech above all else: "It's the freedom that I cherish," says one Anon, "to say what the fuck I want whenever I want" (Anonymous, 2013, p. 126). Another laments the way OpIsrael (a 2013 pro-Palestinian action) diverted focus from OpWCIT, a protest against UN/ITU moves to enlarge its role in global internet governance: OpWCIT concerned "communication and privacy" and these are "the most important thing" (p. 104). Possessive individualism manifests in statements against "any corporation that seeks to limit you whether this be bandwidth caps, restrictions on your files and media or outright censorship" (p. 133), implying equivalence among data caps, copyright, and censorship. But individualism is also countered by a strong anti-leader and anti-celebrity ethic within Anonymous (Coleman, 2011b, p. 4) and widespread disdain for "namefags" and "leaderfags." Certain key operatives accrued celebrity status (under pseudonyms such as Topiary and Sabu), but the movement as a whole values the ethos of the "hive mind."

This suggests a particular mode of collectivism. While Coleman characterizes Anonymous as driven by consensus and "radical democratic decision making" (2012, p. 95), it is less about deliberation than spontaneous "swarming" whereby participants, other than those involved in initial planning, must decide on the spur of the moment whether to join an action. "Populism" may be more apt than "radical democracy" in this context. A confronting slogan of the Anonymous hive mind is "none of us are as cruel as all of us." In Knappenberger's documentary, Anons explicitly define Anonymous as an "emergent phenomenon"—visualized through imagery of birds flying in formation—conjuring spontaneous order out of chaos. Indeed, biological metaphors often feature in Anonymous discourse as they do in cyberlibertarian rhetoric more broadly: beyond the commonly invoked "hive mind," a more arresting image offered by one Anon is that "the internet is a living thing [and] Anonymous is like the chemo for the cancer that threatens [it]" (Anonymous, 2013, p. 126). Such tropes decenter the individual in favor of the complex, organic whole, yet coexist with a strong individualist libertarian ethos within the movement.

## POSITIVE/NEGATIVE LIBERTY

A final polarity within the Anonymous ethos involves positive and negative freedoms. Golumbia's claim that cyberlibertarianism privileges negative liberties is borne out by the sanctification of free speech and privacy and by prominent anti-state rhetoric echoing Barlow's Declaration, pitting government as "dinosaurs" (Anonymous, 2013, p. 19) against the internet's "vibrant marketplace of ideas" (p. 34). But there is again an opposing face. Many of the sources in Olson's book, Knappenberger's documentary and *Anonymous on Anonymous* testify to a sense of empowerment and personal development derived from participating in this "community," having previously felt isolated. Actions related to the Arab Spring fostered solidarity with citizens overseas and the provision of "care packages" (guidance and resources for circumventing censorship and surveillance). Coleman and Golub (2008) have previously explored various 'moral genres' of hacking, comparing for example the almost exclusive focus on negative freedoms exhibited by privacy and encryption-based hacking and a greater focus on positive freedom exhibited by free and open source software (F/OSS) advocates. So too we see concern for both negative *and* positive freedoms within Anonymous. Another example of pursuing positive liberty is the attention given to issues of class, inequality and distributive justice in *Anonymous on Anonymous*. In resonance with the Occupy movement and its discourse of the 99%, several Anons draw attention to issues including student debt, cuts in welfare benefits, poverty, homelessness, and the super-rich (Anonymous, 2013, pp. 186–187). Others point to the greed of the ruling classes and the elites. This may not constitute a developed materialist analysis of class, but we cannot say that the Anonymous movement is blind to issues of social class and economic inequality.

## CONCLUSION

The way this article has sought to characterize Anonymous has implications for assessing its broader political significance. Characterizing Anonymous simply as cyberlibertarian risks overlooking its multiple and even contradictory registers. It could lead to a view that Anonymous has little to contribute and may even be anathema to a progressive politics founded on positive as well as negative freedoms: for example, attention to social justice (including equalizing access to technology) and expanding the digital commons (positive freedoms that require political intervention), in addition to focusing on freedom *from* surveillance, censorship and the expansion of copyright. Libertarian values may be most pronounced, but the contradictory nature of the Anonymous ethos also signals space for a progressive political agenda.

Another way to characterize Anonymous is to emphasize its multiplicity and shape-shifting qualities: Coleman's multiple writings on Anonymous have read Anonymous variously (and plausibly) in terms of Blochian utopianism (2012), proto-Marxian critiques of alienated labor (2011a), market libertarianism and elements of black bloc anarchism (2011c), civil libertarianism and liberalism (2011a), and trickster archetypes (2010). The last of these could, in fact, serve as a container for these various other ways of reading Anonymous and raises the prospect of a "trickster politics" (Coles, 2006) or "insurgent democracy" that "promises a responsiveness, suppleness and mobility that just might develop the power to bring forth a significantly better world" (p. 547). On the other hand, this multiplicity could be viewed negatively as part of what Jodi Dean terms "post-politics." Dean (2012) has diagnosed the Occupy movement's lack of traction as a symptom of its inclusiveness and avoidance of "divisive" politics, eschewing leadership hierarchy and discipline in favor of "emergent" organization. For Dean (following Žižek) post-politics is "politics without politics" (2009). Compared to Occupy, Anonymous *has* embraced a more divisive politics: it does not "fail to take to a stand, to name an enemy" (p. 21). Yet the voices of Anonymous *do* aspire to represent "You, Me, Everybody and Nobody" (Anonymous, 2013, p. 134) and "We, the People" without division along Left and Right (p. 135), transcending the "big ideologies" of the past (p. 8). The point here is not that Anonymous should be dismissed as "post-politics," but rather that focusing too heavily on its amorphous qualities risks obscuring some rather stark polarities within its political ethos and, by extension, its potential contribution to a wider political landscape. As such, this analysis of a series of binary oppositions within the ethos has been offered as a complementary perspective suggesting some contradictory implications.

Both the nihilism *and* the (righteous) idealism of the movement may be somewhat disconnected from a practical agenda for political reform. So too the cloak of an anonymous idea risks obscuring the social identities and material interests underpinning political protest. And yet these facets of Anonymous, together with its playful absurdism, should be seen at least partially in the context of subcultural performance, and not as a fully developed political agenda. Strong utopian and dystopian impulses similarly call into question the movement's capacity to engage with the pragmatics of policy reform, even (or perhaps especially) in the spheres it treats as sacrosanct including online surveillance, privacy, censorship and copyright. And yet these same impulses offer a vital broadening of the narrow political imagination of contemporary mainstream politics. The pronounced individualism of the Anonymous ethos threatens to sanctify privacy, free speech and frictionless data flows at the expense of other goals, and yet the movement has also experimented with (relatively) leaderless collectivism and emphasized the values of solidarity. Finally, the right to be left alone (negative freedom) may be celebrated above all else and yet issues of social justice and economic equality have made inroads into the Anonymous ethos.

Is there a place for hacktivism within a progressive digital politics? The answer is surely yes, if a limited one. The actions and performances of Anonymous have provoked debates over control of digital information, and technology has been deployed to ridicule and draw critical attention to various organizations guilty of dubious practices and abuses of power. These are positive and progressive interventions, even if the long-term impact of Anonymous on the institutions and power structures they have targeted proves to be a limited one.

# REFERENCES

Ackerman, S. (2013, August 6). Former NSA chief warns of cyber-terror attacks if Snowden apprehended. *The Guardian*. Retrieved from http://www.theguardian.com/technology/2013/aug/06/nsa-director-cyber-terrorism-snowden

Allnut, L. (2011). Old-school hacker Oxblood Ruffin discusses Anonymous and the future of hacktivism. Retrieved from http://www.rferl.org/content/hacker_oxblood_ruffin_discusses_anonymous_and_the_future_of_hacktivism/24228166.html

Anonymous. (2013). *Anonymous on Anonymous*. London, England: Imaginary Book Co.

Arthur, C. (2011, July 19). Sun website hacked by LulzSec. *The Guardian*.

Barlow, J. P. (1996). A declaration of the independence of cyberspace. Retrieved from https://projects.eff.org/~barlow/Declaration-Final.html

Bloch, E. (1986). *The principle of hope, Volume 1* (N. Plaice, Trans.). Oxford, England: Blackwell.

Boorsook, P. (2000). *Cyberselfish: A critical romp through the terribly libertarian culture of high tech*. Cambridge, MA: Perseus Books.

Bozzo, S. (Director). (2009). *Hackers wanted* [Documentary]. Retrieved from http://watchdocumentary.org/watch/hackers-wanted-video_c737ec68f.html

Coleman, G. (2010). Hacker and troller as trickster. *Social Text*. Retrieved from http://archive.is/Z9T5

Coleman, G. (2011a). Hacker politics and publics. *Public Culture*, *23*(3), 511–516.

Coleman, G. (2011b). Anonymous: From the Lulz to collective action. *The New Everyday*. Retrieved from http://mediacommons.futureofthebook.org/tne/pieces/anonymous-lulz-collective-action

Coleman, G. (2011c). Is Anonymous anarchy? Retrieved from http://owni.eu/2011/08/22/is-anonymous-anarchy/

Coleman, G. (2012, January). Our weirdness is free: The logic of Anonymous. *Triple Canopy*. Retrieved from http://www.canopycanopycanopy.com/contents/our_weirdness_is_free

Coleman, G. (n.d.). Am I Anonymous? *Limn*, issue 2. Retrieved from http://limn.it/am-i-anonymous/

Coleman, G., & Golub, A. (2008). Hacker practice: Moral genres and the cultural articulation of liberalism. *Anthropological Theory*, *8*(2), 255–277.

Coles, R. (2006). Of tensions and tricksters. Grassroots democracy between theory and practice. *Perspectives on Politics*, *4*(3), 547–561.

Dean, J. (2009). Politics without politics. *Parallax*, *15*(3), 20–36.

Dean, J. (2012). *The communist horizon*. London, England: Verso.

Diamond, M. (1986). Ethics and politics: The American way. In R. Horowitz (Ed.), *The moral foundations of the American republic* (pp. 75–108). Charlottesville, VA: University of Virginia Press.

Fisher, M. (2009). *Capitalist realism: Is there no alternative?* Ropley, England: Zero Books.

Fuchs, C. (2013). The Anonymous movement in the context of liberalism and socialism. *Interface*, *5*(2), 345–376.

Golumbia, D. (2013). Cyberlibertarianism: The extremist foundations of 'digital freedom.' Retrieved from http://www.academia.edu/4429212/Cyberlibertarianism_The_Extremist_Foundations_of_Digital_Freedom

Gordin, M., Tilley, H., & Prakash, G. (2010). Utopia and dystopia beyond space and time. In M. Gordin, H. Tilley, & G. Prakash (Eds.), *Utopia/dystopia: Conditions of historical possibility*. Princeton, NJ: Princeton University Press.

Greenberg, A. (2011). Ex-Anonymous hackers plan to out group's members. Retrieved from http://www.forbes.com/sites/andygreenberg/2011/03/18/ex-anonymous-hackers-plan-to-out-groups-members/

Heclo, H. (2003). The political ethos of George W. Bush. In F. Greenstein (Ed.), *The George W. Bush presidency: An early assessment* (chapter 2). Baltimore, MD: The Johns Hopkins University Press.

Jenkins, J. H. (1991). The state construction of affect: Political ethos and mental health among Salvadoran refugees. *Culture, Medicine and Psychiatry*, *15*(2), 139–165.

Jordan, T. (2008). *Hacking: Digital media and technological determinism*. Cambridge, England: Polity Press.

Knappenberger, B. (Dir. & Writer). (2012). *We are legion: The story of the hacktivists* [documentary]. United States: Luminant Media.

Knuttila, L. (2011). User unknown: 4chan, anonymity and contingency. *First Monday, 16*(10). Retrieved from http://firstmonday.org/ojs/index.php/fm/article/view/3665/3055

Kravets, D. (2010, February 10). Anonymous unfurls 'operation titstorm.' *Wired*. Retrieved from http://www.wired.com/2010/02/anonymous-unfurls-operation-titstorm/

Levitas, R. (2010). *The concept of utopia*. Oxford, England: Peter Lang.

Levy, S. (2010). *Hackers: Heroes of the computer revolution*. Sebastopol, CA: O'Reilly Media.

Limer, E. (2013, January 26). Anonymous attacks department of justice website and threatens worse over Aaron Swartz's suicide. *Gizmodo*. January 26. Retrieved from http://gizmodo.com/5979249/anonymous-attacks-department-of-justice-website-over-aaron-swartzs-suicide

Liu, A. (2004). *The laws of cool: Knowledge work and the culture of information*. Chicago, IL: University of Chicago Press.

Marcuse, H. (1955). *Eros and civilization: A philosophical inquiry into Freud*. Boston, MA: Beacon Press.

Marcuse, H. (1964). *One-dimensional man: Studies in the ideology of advanced industrial society*. Boston, MA: Beacon Press.

Markoff, J. (2011, May 31). Hackers disrupt PBS web site and post a fake report about a rap artist. *New York Times*. Retrieved from http://www.nytimes.com/2011/05/31/technology/31pbs.html?_r=0

Marshall, P. (2008). *Demanding the impossible: A history of anarchism*. London, England: Harper Collins.

Naughton, J. (2000). *A brief history of the future: Origins of the internet*. London, England: Phoenix.

Nietzsche, F. (1968). *Twilight of the idols, and, the Anti-Christ* (R. J. Hollingdale, Trans.). Harmondsworth, England: Penguin.

Norton, Q. (2011, December 26). Antisec hits private intel firm. *Wired*. Retrieved from http://www.wired.com/2011/12/antisec-hits-private-intel-firm-million-of-docs-allegedly-lifted/

Olson, P. (2013). *We are Anonymous: Inside the hacker world of LulzSec, Anonymous and the global cyber insurgency*. London, England: Heinemann.

PBS. (2011). *Frontline: Wikisecrets* [documentary]. Retrieved from http://www.pbs.org/wgbh/pages/frontline/wikileaks/

Stryker, C. (2011). *Epic win for Anonymous: How 4chan's army conquered the web*. New York, NY: Overlook Press.

Taylor, P. (2005). *Hackers* (2nd ed.). London, England: Routledge.

Toffler, A. (1970). *Future shock*. London, England: Bodley Head.

Toffler, A. (1980). *The third wave*. New York, NY: Bantam.

Wilson, J., & Banfield, E. (1971). Political ethos revisited. *The American Political Science Review*, 65(4), 1048–1062.

# Index

INDEX

105

For Product Safety Concerns and Information please contact our EU
representative GPSR@taylorandfrancis.com
Taylor & Francis Verlag GmbH, Kaufingerstraße 24, 80331 München, Germany

www.ingramcontent.com/pod-product-compliance
Ingram Content Group UK Ltd.
Pitfield, Milton Keynes, MK11 3LW, UK
UKHW051830180425
457613UK00022B/1181